Business Cycles
Fact, Fallacy and Fantasy

Sumru G Altug

Koç University, Turkey &
Centre for Economic Policy Research, UK

Business Cycles
Fact, Fallacy and Fantasy

 **World Scientific**

NEW JERSEY · LONDON · SINGAPORE · BEIJING · SHANGHAI · HONG KONG · TAIPEI · CHENNAI

Published by

World Scientific Publishing Co. Pte. Ltd.

5 Toh Tuck Link, Singapore 596224

USA office: 27 Warren Street, Suite 401-402, Hackensack, NJ 07601

UK office: 57 Shelton Street, Covent Garden, London WC2H 9HE

Library of Congress Cataloging-in-Publication Data
Altug, Sumru.
    Business cycles : fact, fallacy, and fantasy / by Sumru G. Altug.
        p. cm.
    Includes bibliographical references and index.
    ISBN-13: 978-981-283-276-4 (hardcover)
    ISBN-10: 981-283-276-9 (hardcover)
    1: Business cycles. I. Title.
    HB3711.A424 2009
    338.5'42--dc22
                                            2009034620

British Library Cataloguing-in-Publication Data
A catalogue record for this book is available from the British Library.

Typeset by Stallion Press
Email: enquiries@stallionpress.com

Printed in Singapore by World Scientific Printers

Preface

How do intellectual disciplines progress? Undoubtedly, the discipline of economics — and macroeconomics, in particular — is affected by major changes in economic conditions. The Great Depression greatly influenced the perceptions of a generation of economists, beginning with Keynes. The oil shocks of the 1970s and the 1980s affected economists' views regarding the sources of macroeconomic fluctuations.

Sometimes, the development of new techniques or new ways of modeling can also affect the course that a discipline takes. Large-scale computers in the post-World War II era played an important role in the development of simultaneous equation models. In recent years, real business cycle (RBC) analysis has come to provide a flexible and popular approach for examining macroeconomic phenomena. In 2004, Finn Kydland and Edward Prescott received the Nobel Prize in Economics, and The Royal Swedish Academy of Sciences published a report titled *Finn Kydland and Edward Prescott's Contribution to Dynamic Macroeconomics: The Time Consistency of Economic Policy and the Driving Forces Behind Business Cycles* [204]. The field of macroeconomics has changed significantly due to Kydland and Prescott's contributions.

This book draws upon Kydland and Prescott's original contribution. I was a Ph.D. student at the Graduate School of Industrial Administration at Carnegie Mellon University when Kydland and Prescott's "Time-to-Build and Aggregate Fluctuations" article was published in the early 1980s [141]. My thesis was on estimating the model in the same article. The model was rejected, much to the delight of macroeconomists of a more Keynesian bent! Yet many felt that economic models should be subject to formal econometric and statistical testing. This debate continues to this day.

Kydland and Prescott's seminal article initiated the school of RBC analysis. This literature evolved in different ways. Talented and creative individuals extended the initial Kydland–Prescott research in different ways. Not content with the initial rejection of the model, many researchers also pursued the econometric analysis of RBC models. In recent years, researchers at central banks have begun using so-called dynamic stochastic general equilibrium (DSGE) models for policy analysis.

This book attempts to provide an overview of the burgeoning business cycle literature that, in many ways, reflects my own interests. There have been a number of excellent publications that have examined different facets of this literature. The volume by Thomas Cooley [74] can be considered a primer of RBC analysis and its applications. James Hartley, Kevin Hoover, and Kevin Salyer's [116] collection of articles provides a critique of the calibration approach. Jordi Gali's [97] recent text articulates an alternative New Keynesian framework for describing aggregate fluctuations. This book takes a more eclectic approach, asking some basic questions about RBC analysis and summarizing the ongoing controversies surrounding it.

Contents

Chapter 1
Introduction

In the opening page of the book *Business Cycles* published in 1927, Wesley Mitchell [163] comments as thus: "As knowledge of business cycles grows, more effort is required to master it." Ever since, there have been many developments in the field of business cycles. This book describes these new developments.

Historically, the notion of business cycles originated from various types of panics, depressions, and crises experienced by market economies in the 19th and early 20th centuries. According to Karl Marx, one of the most prominent thinkers of the time, "crises" are an endemic feature of capitalist economies. As Mitchell [163] recounts, much effort was devoted to understanding the causes of what many viewed as "abnormal" phenomena. However, other economists observed that the alternating phases of prosperity and depression seemed to follow each other on a regular basis, when one examined the history of commercial cycles for the capitalist economies of the time. In the 1920s, Kondratiev [137] argued that in addition to shorter economic cycles, there were periodic movements or "long waves" in economic variables. Schumpeter [187, 188] sought to explain the existence of such long waves as an outcome of technological innovations. In his framework, both growth and business cycles could be ascribed to the process of innovation. He identified three long waves: 1780–1840, corresponding to the Industrial Revolution; 1840–1890, corresponding to the introduction of steel and steam engines; and 1890–1950, corresponding to the invention of electricity, chemical processing, and motor engines.

While some scholars proposed different theories to explain fluctuations in economic activity, other scholars investigated methods for the systematic measurement and identification of business cycles. During this time, Burns and Mitchell [50] and researchers at the National Bureau of Economic Research (NBER) began to identify the phenomena of business cycles. According to them, a business cycle is the simultaneous downturns and upturns of a large number of economic series. Their work involved the dating of business cycles and the development of leading indicators for the US economy, and it continues to this day in the business cycle dating methodology employed by the NBER.[1] We discuss the NBER methodology and the stylized facts of business cycles in Chapter 2.

Another important channel which affected the study of business cycles was the development of statistical and time series methods. Writers such as Frisch and Slutsky embedded the notion of business cycles into simple dynamic systems driven by stochastic shocks. Their influence on thinking about business cycles has persisted to this day. The Norwegian economist Ragnar Frisch [95] developed the notions of impulse and propagation mechanisms for describing business cycles, and modeled business cycles as the response of a second-order dynamic system to random shocks. Slutsky [193] argued that the sum of a number of uncorrelated shocks could produce serially correlated or smooth movements in the generated series. Their ideas were formulated in terms of linear time series models, which continue to form the main vehicle for empirically studying business cycles.

The Great Depression and World War II were two major events in the development of business cycle analysis. The period following World War II was an era of high and sustained growth in many countries. Nevertheless, the lessons of the Great Depression were vivid in the minds of many policy-makers. After the early work of Burns and Mitchell, post World War II, the focus shifted to stabilization policy. Keynes' *General Theory* [127] laid the foundations for the analysis of short-run economic fluctuations. Post World War II, the Keynesian framework was interpreted as a model of output determination at a point in time. The oil shocks of the 1970s and the experience of high inflation and high unemployment, or *stagflation* as it is popularly known, led researchers to account for the observations using new mechanisms for the effects of money on output. In their seminal contributions, Phelps [170] and Lucas [148, 149] developed monetary models of the business cycle as a way

---

[1] See also Zarnowitz [211].

of providing a consistent theoretical foundation for describing the impact of changes in money on output. In Phelps' and Lucas' framework, the emphasis was on generating the Phillips-curve type of phenomena between inflation and unemployment based on informational frictions. Despite providing great theoretical advances in the analysis of aggregative phenomena, the specific mechanisms postulated in this literature as leading to business cycles, namely, unanticipated shocks to money, failed to garner sufficient empirical support.

During this period, there was a revival of interest more generally in examining aggregate economic activity as recurrent phenomena characterizing the functioning of economies with optimizing agents. In his article "Understanding Business Cycles", Lucas [151] cataloged the remarkable conformity in a set of economic series and set forth an agenda for explaining these facts using an *equilibrium* approach. Lucas and Rapping [153] argued that observed fluctuations in aggregate labor supply could be modeled as the voluntary response of agents based on intertemporal substitution effects. Long and Plosser [147] developed a simple Robinson Crusoe economy and generated many of the characteristics of modern macroeconomic time series through the mechanisms of substitution and wealth effects in response to technology shocks affecting different sectors of the economy. The literature on real business cycle (RBC) theory owes its existence to Kydland and Prescott [141], who presented a model that featured technology shocks as the main impulse behind cyclical fluctuations and proposed a rich array of propagation mechanisms for these shocks, namely, the durability of leisure, time-to-build in investment, and inventories. They also proposed a methodology for confronting their theory with the data. Widely known as the *calibration* approach, this involves matching a small set of moments implied by the model with those in the data. Though this approach is cited extensively, the merits of this approach have been a topic of debate. We will discuss RBC models further in Chapter 3.

Since this book purports to discuss business cycles, we cannot ignore the calibration approach or, more generally, the debate on the empirical validation of business cycle models. One of the major issues with Kydland and Prescott's contribution, as identified by skeptics, was identifying technology shocks that could generate cyclical fluctuations of magnitudes observed in the data (see Summers [202]). In some sense, this feature of Kydland and Prescott's analysis was viewed as "fantastical" by many. Other skeptics contested the implications of the RBC approach for the observed behavior of productivity. Productivity, or the Solow residual, is known to be *procyclical*. According to the RBC approach, the observed procyclical movements in productivity should merely be a response to exogenous technology shocks (see Prescott [173]). In a series of papers, Hall [110, 111] argued persuasively that there were most likely endogenous components to the cyclical movement of productivity arising from imperfect competition at the firm level and internal increasing returns to scale in production. A deeper problem lay in modeling the movement of economy-wide averages (possibly fallaciously) in terms of the behavior of a representative or stand-in household.

Subsequent research that evolved from the original Kydland–Prescott exercise has proceeded along several different dimensions. On the one hand, a plethora of papers have presented modifications to the original Kydland–Prescott framework to reconcile the model with many of the actual features of the data. For example, the original Kydland–Prescott model could not explain the relative variability of hours and productivity or real wages. It also failed to account for the correlation between hours and productivity. The model lacked money; hence, it faced the problem of reconciling observations on money–output correlations within a model where the main driving force was real productivity shocks. Many of these issues have taken on the character of "puzzles" in the RBC literature, and they have constituted the topic for much further study. The RBC literature has also generated international business cycle models to replicate findings on current account dynamics, international risk sharing, financial diversification, and international capital flows. More recently, models have been developed that study the role of market completeness/incompleteness on cyclical fluctuations (see, for example, Heathcote and Perri [117]). The original RBC framework has also been extended in recent years to examine the business cycle phenomena in emerging market economies. We will examine a few of these directions in later chapters.

A more general critique to RBC analysis was mounted by the New Keynesian challenge. The New Keynesian viewpoint breaks with the RBC approach by contesting the view that prices adjust frictionlessly to clear markets. Instead, it introduces alternative mechanisms for generating price stickiness such as imperfect competition among firms, markups, endogenous changes in efficiency due to increasing returns to scale, and variable factor utilization. The New Keynesian challenge has proceeded along theoretical lines (see Rotemberg and Woodford [182]) and empirical considerations (see Gali [96] or Basu, Fernald, and Kimball [32]). This facilitates the analysis of the different effects of government versus technology shocks, or monetary versus technology shocks. We will discuss New Keynesian models in detail in Chapter 5.

The controversy over the calibration approach also resulted in work on alternative methods for empirically analyzing business cycle phenomena. One approach that is popular in the business cycle literature is the method of unobservable index models or dynamic factor analysis developed by Sargent and Sims [185] and others. Following Sims [191], vector autoregression (VAR) and structural VAR (SVAR) have also proven to be popular in empirical macroeconomic research. While both models allow for rich dynamic interrelationships among a set of endogenous variables and an examination of business cycle dynamics based on impulse response functions, SVAR also permits an identification of shocks. More recently, dynamic stochastic general equilibrium (DSGE) models have been developed to identify shocks and propagation mechanisms of business cycles models (see, for example, Smets and Wouters [194, 195]).[2] We will discuss the issues involved in matching the model with the data in Chapter 7.

---

[2]Canova [58] is an excellent reference source on the quantitative and empirical analysis of dynamic stochastic general equilibrium models.

Chapter 2

Facts

The vast literature on business cycles has focused on generating the stylized facts regarding cyclical fluctuations. Mitchell [163], Mitchell and Burns [164], and Burns and Mitchell [50] provide a framework to describe the main features of business cycles. This framework is based on the principle of identifying turning points in economic activity and determining which series constitute leading, coincident, or lagging indicators of the business cycle. Stock and Watson [197] present a modern methodology to describe business cycles in terms of the cyclical time series behavior of the main macroeconomic series and their co-movement with cyclical output. In this chapter, we describe the National Bureau of Economic Research (NBER) methodology for dating business cycles and present the basic facts regarding business cycles.

Much of the early work on business cycles was implemented for the US economy. However, the European or euro area business cycle has also been the topic of much recent study (see Artis, Kontolemis, and Osborn [20], Artis and Zhang [18], and Stock and Watson [199], among others). Basu and Taylor [31] have examined business cycles in an international historical context. We will also discuss some of the empirical findings in these regards.

2.1. DEFINING A BUSINESS CYCLE

The notion that market economies are subject to recurring fluctuations in a large set of variables was formalized by Burns and Mitchell [50] in their 1946 work entitled *Measuring Business Cycles* as follows:

> Business cycles are a type of fluctuation found in the aggregate economic activity of nations that organize their work mainly in business enterprises; a cycle consists of expansions occurring at about the same time in many

economic activities, followed by similarly general recessions, contractions, and revivals which merge into the expansion phase of the next cycle; this sequence of changes is recurrent but not periodic; in duration business cycles vary from one year to ten or twelve years; they are not divisible into shorter cycles of similar cycles with amplitudes approximating their own.

This definition has formed the basis of modern thinking about business cycles, whether it pertains to the measurement of business cycles or the construction of models of cyclical fluctuations.

Burns and Mitchell [50] themselves noted that this definition raised as many questions as it sought to answer. Some of these questions are precisely the ones that we seek to answer in this book. If one talks about "fluctuations in the aggregate economic activity of nations", then should one worry about differences in business cycle activity across regions? Should business cycles be considered in an international context? How about the historical nature of business cycles? Have business cycles moderated over time? Likewise, when one considers the statement regarding expansions occurring in "many economic activities", how broadly should the aggregates that are being considered be defined? The notion that changes in economic activity occur "at about the same time" admit the possibility of economic variables that lead or lag the cycle. In seeking to identify "recurrent changes", how should we deal with seasonal changes, random fluctuations, or secular trends? Finally, the comments regarding the duration and amplitude of business cycles are based on actual observations of cyclical phenomena, and also lay down rules for excluding irregular movements and other similar changes.

The NBER approach to identifying business cycles as outlined by Mitchell [163], Mitchell and Burns [164], and Burns and Mitchell [50] is comprised of two mutually reinforcing acts: first, find the cyclical peaks and troughs in a given set of economic variables; and second, determine whether these turning points are sufficiently common across the series. If the answer to the latter question is in the affirmative, then an aggregate business cycle or a *reference cycle* is identified. Once the reference dates are found, the cyclical behavior of each series is then examined relative to the reference cycle. As part of this analysis, the duration, timing, and amplitude of each specific cycle are compared with that of the reference cycle. Burns and Mitchell [50] stress that the notion of a reference cycle should not be equated with an observable construct. In their words (Burns and Mitchell [50], Ch. 2, p. 14):

When we speak of 'observing' business cycles we use figurative language. For, like other concepts, business cycles can be seen only 'in the mind's eye'. What we literally observe is not a congeries of economic activities rising and falling in unison, but changes in readings taken from many recording instruments of varying reliability.

The NBER business cycle methodology identifies a business cycle based on the (absolute) downturn of the level of output. This is known as a *classical business cycle*. There is an alternative approach which considers the decline in the series measured as a deviation from its long-run trend. Following the terminology in Zarnowitz [211], such cycles are known as *growth cycles*. One advantage of using growth cycles is that they have expansions and contractions that are approximately of the same duration. By contrast, classical cycles typically have recessions that are shorter than expansions because of the growth effect. Figure 2.1 displays the difference between classical and growth cycles. Point A defines a *trough* for a classical cycle while point B defines a *peak*. By contrast, a trough occurs at point C for a growth cycle while point D defines a peak. When the economy is moving from a trough to a peak, we say that it is

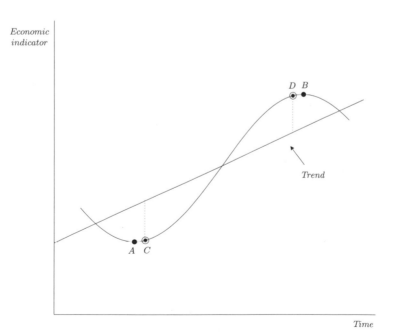

Fig. 2.1.   Classical and Growth Cycles.

in an *expansion*, and a *recession* is said to occur when the economy is moving from a peak to a trough. The *duration* of the business cycle is the length of time (in months, quarters, or years) that the economy spends between two troughs or, equivalently, two peaks. The *amplitude* of a business cycle is the deviation from trend.

The dating of business cycles for the US is done formally by the NBER Business Cycle Dating Committee. This committee uses data on real output, national income, employment, and trade at the sectoral and aggregate levels to identify and date business cycles. The turning points are determined judgmentally, although a computer algorithm exists that can approximate the results (see Bry and Boschan [49]). As an example, this committee recently announced that the US economy had formally been in a recession since December 2007. Table 2.1 gives the dates of business cycles or the so-called "reference dates" for the US economy since 1857. There are 32 complete cycles in the entire sample period. The average length of a cycle (peak from previous peak or trough from previous trough) in the post-WWII era is 67 months or over five years. The shortest cycle is 17 months or nearly six quarters, and the longest cycle is 128 months or more than ten years. We can also observe expansionary and contractionary phases of the business cycle from this table. Post WWII, the average length of a contraction has decreased to ten months from 17 months or more in the years preceding 1945. Similarly, the average length of an expansion has increased to 57 months from, at most, 38 months pre-WWII. One of the longest expansions to have occurred post-WWII is between March 1991 and November 2001 — a period of 120 months. This period was dubbed as the period of the "Great Moderation".

If one chooses to use growth cycles, there is an issue of how to identify the cyclical component of a given series. As King, Plosser, Stock, and Watson [133] argue, real business cycle (RBC) models which allow for trends in the technology shock imply that growth and business cycles are jointly determined. Nevertheless, the practice of separating the trend and cyclical component using linear time series methods is well established. There are several approaches to de-trending economic time series. One approach is to use a linear de-trending procedure which assumes that the underlying series possesses deterministic time trends. An alternative approach is to assume a stochastic trend modeled as a unit root in the series at hand. The contribution of Nelson and Plosser [167] was to show that economic time series such as real GDP typically possess unit roots. However, in their survey of empirical business cycles, Stock and

Table 2.1. US Business Cycle Expansions and Contractions.

Business Cycle Reference Dates		Duration in Months			
		Contraction	Expansion	Cycle	Cycle
Peak	Trough	Peak to Trough	Previous Trough to This Peak	Trough from Previous Trough	Peak from Previous Peak
	December 1854 (IV)	—	—	—	—
June 1857(II)	December 1858 (IV)	18	30	48	—
October 1860(III)	June 1861 (III)	8	22	30	40
April 1865(I)	December 1867 (I)	32	46	78	54
June 1869(II)	December 1870 (IV)	18	18	36	50
October 1873(III)	March 1879 (I)	65	34	99	52
March 1882(I)	May 1885 (II)	38	36	74	101
March 1887(II)	April 1888 (I)	13	22	35	60
July 1890(III)	May 1891 (II)	10	27	37	40
January 1893(I)	June 1894 (II)	17	20	37	30
December 1895(IV)	June 1897 (II)	18	18	36	35
June 1899(III)	December 1900 (IV)	38	24	42	42
September 1902(IV)	August 1904 (III)	23	21	44	39
May 1907(II)	June 1908 (II)	13	33	46	56
January 1910(I)	January 1912 (IV)	24	19	43	32
January 1913(I)	December 1914 (IV)	23	12	35	36
August 1918(III)	March 1919 (I)	7	44	51	67
January 1920(I)	July 1921 (III)	18	10	28	17
May 1923(II)	July 1924 (III)	14	22	36	40
October 1926(III)	November 1927 (IV)	13	27	40	41
August 1929(III)	March 1933 (I)	43	21	64	34

(*Continued*)

Table 2.1. (*Continued*)

Business Cycle Reference Dates		Duration in Months			
		Contraction	Expansion	Cycle	
Peak	Trough	Peak to Trough	Previous Trough to This Peak	Trough from Previous Trough	Peak from Previous Peak
May 1937(II)	June 1938 (II)	13	50	63	93
February 1945(I)	October 1945 (IV)	8	80	88	93
November 1948(IV)	October 1949 (IV)	11	37	48	45
July 1953(II)	May 1954 (II)	10	45	55	56
August 1957(III)	April 1958 (II)	8	39	47	49
April 1960(II)	February 1961 (I)	10	24	34	32
December 1969(IV)	November 1970 (IV)	11	106	117	116
November 1973(IV)	March 1975 (I)	16	36	52	47
January 1980(I)	July 1980 (III)	6	58	64	74
July 1981(III)	November 1982 (IV)	16	12	20	18
July 1990(III)	March 1991(I)	8	92	100	108
March 2001(I)	November 2001 (IV)	8	120	128	128
December 2007 (IV)			73		81
Average, all cycles:					
1854–2001 (32 cycles)		17	38	55	56*
1854–1919 (16 cycles)		22	27	48	49**
1919–1945 (6 cycles)		18	35	53	53
1945–2001 (10 cycles)		10	57	67	67

*13 cycles; **15 cycles.
Source: NBER.

Watson [197] argue that neither linear time trends nor first-differencing to eliminate unit roots provides a satisfactory approach to identifying the cyclical component of a series. The first approach tends to generate spurious business cycle effects in the de-trended series, whereas the second exacerbates the role of short-term noise.

Several alternative approaches have been proposed in the recent business cycle literature to separate the trend versus cyclical component of a time series. One of these approaches is the so-called Hodrick–Prescott [120] (HP) filter, which involves minimizing a quadratic form to determine the trend component in a given series. Specifically, let y_t denote the series in question and g_t denote the unknown trend component. The Hodrick–Prescott filter defines g_t to solve

$$\min_{g_t} \sum_{t=-\infty}^{\infty} (y_t - g_t)^2 + \mu \sum_{t=-\infty}^{\infty} \left[(g_{t+1} - g_t) - (g_t - g_{t-1}) \right]^2 .$$

The cyclical component of the series is defined as $y_t^c = y_t - g_t$. The parameter μ controls the smoothness of the trend component. For quarterly data, μ is typically recorded as 1600. Taking the derivative with respect to g_t yields

$$\sum_{t=-\infty}^{\infty} \left[\mu g_{t+2} - 4\mu g_{t+1} + (1 + 6\mu)g_t - 4\mu g_{t-1} + \mu g_{t-2} \right] = \sum_{t=-\infty}^{\infty} y_t.$$

$$(1.1)$$

Using the lag operator notation and simplifying, the cyclical component can be represented as

$$y_t^c = y_t - g_t = \frac{\mu(1 - L^{-1})^2(1 - L)^2}{1 + \mu(1 - L^{-1})^2(1 - L)^2} y_t. \qquad (1.2)$$

In practice, the filter is applied using a finite sample. The general equation characterizing the filter, Eq. (1.1), is modified at the beginning and end of the sample. The properties of the HP filter have been studied by many authors, including Singleton [192], King and Rebelo [130], and Cogley and Nason [69]. Cogley and Nason have argued, in particular, that business cycle dynamics obtained by using a HP de-trending procedure depend on the properties of the underlying data. If these are trend-stationary, then the de-trending procedure has favorable properties; if the underlying data are difference-stationary, however, application of the HP filter induces spurious business cycle fluctuations.

A second approach is based on the spectral analysis of economic time series. The *band-pass filter* developed by Baxter and King [37] "filters" out both the long-run trend and the high-frequency movements in a given time series while retaining those components associated with periodicities of typical business cycle durations, namely, periodicities between six quarters and eight years. The band-pass filter of Baxter and King [37] is obtained by applying a Kth-order moving average to a given time series:

$$y_t^* = \sum_{k=K}^{K} a_k y_{t-k},\tag{1.3}$$

where the moving average coefficients are chosen to be symmetric, $a_k = a_{-k}$ for $k = 1, \ldots, K$. They show that if the sum of the moving average coefficients is zero, $\sum_{k=K}^{K} a_k = 0$, then it has trend elimination properties. In particular, they show that the lag polynomial describing the Kth-order moving average can be written as

$$a(L) = (1 - L)(1 - L^{-1})\psi(L),\tag{1.4}$$

where $\psi(L)$ is a $(K-1)$-order symmetric moving average polynomial. Hence, the Baxter–King filter will eliminate deterministic quadratic trends or render stationary series that are integrated up to order two, i.e, $I(2)$ or less. The filter is designed to have a number of other properties, including the property that the results should not depend on the sample size and that it does not alter the timing relations between series at any frequency. Baxter and King derive the band-pass filter by considering low-pass and high-pass filters with the required properties. Let s denote the number of observations in a year. The band-pass filter retains the movements in a series for the frequencies associated with the periodicities of $0.5s$ and $8s$. The frequency response function of the ideal band-pass filter is defined as

$$\beta_{bp}(\omega) = I(2\pi/(8s) \leq \omega \leq 2\pi/(0.5s)),$$

where $I(\cdot)$ is the indicator function. It turns out that the time-domain representation of the band-pass filter is an infinite moving average. However, once the ideal filter's weights are found in the time domain, the optimal

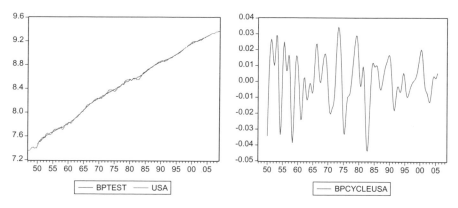

Fig. 2.2. Trend and Cyclical Components in USA GDP.

approximating filter with maximum lag K is obtained by truncating the ideal filter's weights at lag K. Baxter and King [37] employ a finite-order approximation to obtain the coefficients of this filter with a truncation of $K = 3$ years or $K = 12$ quarters. In what follows, we use this approach to generate the cyclical components of the different series.

Figure 2.2 illustrates the logarithm of real GDP for the US and its trend and components estimated according to the Baxter–King filter for the period 1947(I)–2005(III). We observe that real GDP displays a marked positive trend over the sample period, showing the large gains in productivity and growth attained over this period. We also observe the cyclical troughs and peaks of economic activity associated with the business cycle. We can observe the cyclical downturns and upturns corresponding to the NBER business cycle reference dates from this graph. The cyclical component tracks very well the US business cycle as identified by the NBER. Nevertheless, the notion of a "business cycle" is also concerned with the co-movement of a large number of economic variables. Section 2.2 discusses these properties of business cycles.

2.2. STYLIZED FACTS

In this section, we provide some stylized facts of business cycles. These facts constitute important benchmarks by which to judge the performance of alternative models of business cycles. We consider a measure of the business cycle as the co-movement of the cyclical behavior of individual series with the cyclical component of real output. According to this approach, variables that move in the same direction over the cycle as real output are *procyclical*. Variables that move in the opposite direction (rise during recessions and fall in expansions) are *countercyclical*. Variables that display little correlation with output over the cycle are called *acyclical*. We can also examine whether different time series are out of phase with real GDP. For example, a leading indicator reaches a peak before real GDP reaches its peak and bottoms out (reaches a trough) before real GDP. Leading indicators are useful for predicting subsequent changes in real GDP. Coincident indicators reach a peak or a trough at roughly the same time as real GDP. Finally, lagging indicators reach a peak or trough after real GDP.

The stylized facts of business cycles are typically defined in terms of the behavior of the **main components of GDP**, **hours**, **productivity**, **real wages**, **asset returns and prices**, and **monetary aggregates**. These have been described in a number of economic studies.[1] Information on leading indicators is also collected by the Conference Board.[2]

The salient facts of a business cycle can be described as follows:

1. Real output across virtually all sectors of the economy moves together. In other words, the contemporaneous correlation of output in different sectors of the economy is large and positive. Exceptions are production of agricultural goods and natural resources, which are not especially procyclical.

2. Consumption, investment, inventories, and imports are all strongly procyclical. Consumption of durables is much more volatile than consumption of nondurable goods and services. Consumption of

---

[1] Stock and Watson [197] use data on 71 variables to characterize US business cycle phenomena over the period 1953–1996. They make use of the Baxter–King band-pass filter to identify the trend versus cyclical components of each series. Among other measures, they consider the co-movement of the cyclical component of GDP with the cyclical component of each series, and the cross-correlations of the cyclical component of GDP with the cyclical component of each series for lags and leads up to six periods. Backus and Kehoe [23] analyze the properties of historical business cycles for ten developed countries using a century-long dataset up to the 1980s. They use the HP filter to derive the cyclical components of the different series, and separate their sample period into the pre-World War I era, the interwar era between World War I and II, and the post-World War II era.

[2] Early work on developing a composite index of leading indicators is due to Mitchell and Burns [164]. Such a composite index was made official by the US Department of Commerce in 1968, and passed over to the Conference Board in 1995.

durable goods fluctuates more than GDP, whereas nondurables fluctuate considerably less.

3. Investment in equipment and nonresidential structures is procyclical with a lag. Investment in residential structures is procyclical and highly volatile.

4. Government spending tends to be acyclical. The correlation between government expenditures and output is nearly zero.

5. Net exports are countercyclical. The correlation with output is generally negative, but weakly so. Since imports are more strongly procyclical than exports, the trade balance tends to be countercyclical.

6. Total employment, employee hours, and capacity utilization are all strongly procyclical. The employment series lags the business cycle by a quarter, while capacity utilization tends to be coincident.

7. Employment fluctuates almost as much as output and total hours of work, while average weekly hours fluctuate much less. The implication is that most fluctuations in total hours result from movements in and out of the work force rather than adjustments in average hours of work.

8. Real wages are procyclical or acyclical. They have not displayed a steady pattern in terms of variability to GDP or in terms of leading, coincident, or lagging indicators.

9. Productivity is slightly procyclical, but both real wages and productivity vary considerably less than output.

10. Profits are highly volatile.

11. Nominal interest rates tend to be procyclical. The yield curve which shows the rates of return on bonds of different maturities tends to be upward-sloping during an expansion and downward-sloping at the onset of a recession. That is, an expansion is characterized by expectations of higher interest rates at longer horizons whereas a recession typically signals a decline in long-term interest rates relative to short-term rates, namely, an inverted yield curve.

12. Velocity and the money supply are procyclical.

13. The risk premium for holding private debt, or the yield spread between corporate paper and Treasury bills with six months' maturity, tends to shrink during expansions and increase during recessions. The reason for this countercyclical behavior is likely to be changes in default risk.

14. The stock market is positively related to the subsequent growth rate of real GDP. In this sense, changes in stock prices have been taken as providing information about the future course of the real economy. Between 1945 and 1980, the stock market fell in the quarter before each of the eight recessions, although it is important to emphasize that the market has fallen without a subsequent recession.

15. Money (M2) is procyclical and tends to be a leading indicator of output. However, the procyclicality of M2 has diminished since the 1980s.

16. The behavior of prices and inflation appears to have changed over time. In the pre-WWI period and interwar period, inflation was procyclical with a very low mean. Since the early 1980s, inflation appears to be countercyclical. A similar change appears to have characterized the behavior of price-level fluctuations.

17. The standard deviation of inflation is lower than that of real GDP.

18. Inflation is a coincident indicator.

19. There is also a marked increase in the persistence of inflation after WWII.

20. Finally, contemporaneous correlations between output fluctuations in different countries were highest in the interwar period, reflecting the common experience of the Great Depression, with the exception of Germany and Japan. The correlation is typically larger in the post-war period than in the pre-war period.

This set of facts constitutes a benchmark which a successful business cycle model should meet. The findings concerning the behavior of hours, employment, real wages, and productivity have proved among the most difficult to reconcile by current business cycle theories. The changes in the cyclical behavior of prices and inflation also have implications for the so-called impulses and propagation mechanisms of business cycles. In the post-WWII era, there is more evidence of supply-side-driven fluctuations in output. Witness the impact of the large oil shocks in the 1970s, a topic to which we will return; hence, the increased persistence of inflation and the countercyclical behavior of prices observed in this era. By contrast, prices and inflation were procyclical in the pre-WWII era. One way to rationalize this phenomenon may be in terms of monetary policy that is more accommodative — under a gold standard, for example. Other papers have generated business cycle facts using data over long samples. Chadha and Nolan [62] identify the stylized facts of business cycles for the UK economy over a long sample period. A'Hearna and Woitek [2] establish the facts of business cycles in the late 19th century using spectral techniques.

The above findings can also shed light on whether output fluctuations have moderated in the post-WWII era. On the one hand, Christina Romer [180, 181] has argued that the finding of lower output variability in the post-WWII period is due to changes in the measurement of output in the pre- and post-WWII eras. If the higher-quality data in the post-WWII period are subjected to a transformation that makes the pre- and post-WWII data of comparable quality, then one discerns *no* change in output fluctuations across the two periods. While her findings have garnered much interest, Backus and Kehoe [23] argue that it is difficult to reach a firm conclusion on this point based on US data alone. They suggest that if one considers additional evidence based on a larger sample of countries over the different periods, the variability of output appears to have diminished in the post-WWII period. Stock and Watson [198] seek to avoid the problem of poor data quality in the pre-WWII period, and compare the volatility of 21 different variables in the 20 years since the 1980s and the 40 years in the period following WWII up to the 1980s. They find that the standard deviations of a typical variable in their sample declined by about 20–40% since the 1980s. They attribute around 20–30% of the reduction in output volatility to better monetary policy, 15% to smaller shocks to productivity, and another 15% to reduced shocks to food and commodity prices. Their findings also provide evidence on the factors behind the "Great Moderation".

2.3. THE EURO AREA BUSINESS CYCLE

Much of the early work on the European business cycle was concerned with examining the impact of monetary union arrangements on economic activity. Artis and Zhang [18, 19] investigate the relationship of the European Exchange Rate Mechanism (ERM) to the international business cycle in terms of the linkage and synchronization of cyclical fluctuations between countries. Their findings suggest the emergence of a group-specific European business cycle since the formation of the ERM, which is independent of the US cycle. Artis, Kontolemis, and Osborn [20] propose business cycle turning points for a number of countries based on industrial production. The countries selected are the G7 countries along with the prominent European countries. They use this information to examine the international nature of cyclical movements, and to determine whether cyclical movements are similar across different countries. They also consider the lead/lag relationships between countries at peaks and troughs.

Artis, Marcellino, and Proietti [21] discuss alternative approaches to dating euro area business cycles. As in the Stock and Watson [197] approach, they distinguish between classical and growth cycles. The euro area experience makes consideration of both types of business cycles relevant. Whereas in the post-WWII era the euro area countries exhibited high rates of growth, making growth cycles the relevant concept, in recent years growth has slowed and even absolute declines in real GDP have been observed, implying that classical cycles should also be considered. These authors also articulate a formal model of turning points based on restrictions imposed on a Markov process.[3] To describe this algorithm, suppose that the economy can be in one of two mutually exclusive states, *expansion* E_t or *recession* R_t. Suppose that a peak terminates an expansion, and a trough terminates a recession. The Markov process distinguishes between turning points within the two states by assuming that

$$E_t = \begin{cases} EC_t & \text{expansion continuation} \\ P_t & \text{peak} \end{cases},$$

$$R_t = \begin{cases} RC_t & \text{recession continuation} \\ T_t & \text{trough} \end{cases}.$$

Let $p_{EP} = Pr(P_{t+1}|EC_t)$ denote the probability of transiting to a peak, conditional on being in an expansion, which implies that the probability of continuing an expansion $p_{EE} = Pr(EC_{t+1}|EC_t)$ is given by $p_{EE} = 1 - p_{EP}$. Likewise, define $p_{RT} = Pr(T_{t+1}|RC_t)$ as the probability of transiting to a trough, conditional on being in a contraction. Then, the probability of continuing a contraction $p_{RR} = Pr(RC_{t+1}|RC_t)$ is $p_{RR} = 1 - p_{RT}$. Let S_t denote a discrete random variable that follows a first-order Markov process

---

[3]This algorithm follows Harding and Pagan [115], who extended the Bry and Boschan [49] algorithm to a quarterly setting.

with four states and transition probability matrix as follows:

	EC_{t+1}	P_{t+1}	RC_{t+1}	T_{t+1}
EC_t	p_{EE}	p_{EP}	0	0
P_t	0	0	1	0
RC_t	0	0	p_{RR}	p_{RT}
T_t	1	0	0	0

The dating rules impose minimum durations on a phase, expansion or contraction, and on complete cycles, peak-to-peak or trough-to-trough. The duration of a phase is required to be two quarters, which is automatically satisfied since the states (EC_t, P_t) both belong to an expansion and (RC_t, T_t) belong to a contraction. The minimum duration of a complete cycle is given as five quarters. Hence, a peak at date $t - 4$, P_{t-4}, can only be followed by a peak at $t + 1$, P_{t+1}. A similar condition exists for troughs.

Now consider applying this algorithm to dating classical cycles. Let y_t denote the underlying series. Then, we can define an expansion termination sequence, ETS_t, and a recession termination sequence, RTS_t, respectively, as follows:

$$ETS_t = \{(\Delta y_{t+1} < 0) \cup (\Delta^2 y_{t+2} < 0)\}$$
$$RTS_t = \{(\Delta y_{t+1} > 0) \cup (\Delta^2 y_{t+2} > 0)\}.$$

Thus, $\Delta y_{t+1} = y_{t+1} - y_t < 0$ and $\Delta^2 y_{t+2} = y_{t+2} - y_t < 0$ represent the candidate sequence for terminating an expansion, which defines a peak. Likewise, $\Delta y_{t+1} = y_{t+1} - y_t > 0$ and $\Delta^2 y_{t+2} = y_{t+2} - y_t > 0$ represent the candidate sequence for terminating a contraction, which defines a trough. The algorithm is completed by finding the probability that the economy will transit to a peak, conditional on having been in an expansionary phase, p_{EP}. This is the joint event that the history at time t, $(S_{t-4}, S_{t-3}, S_{t-2}, S_{t-1}, S_t)$, features an expansionary state at time t, $S_t = EC_t$, and that ETS_t is true. Else, if ETS_t is false, the expansion continues. Likewise, the probability that the economy will transit to a trough, conditional on having been in a contractionary phase, is p_{RT}. This is the joint event that the history at time t, $(S_{t-4}, S_{t-3}, S_{t-2}, S_{t-1}, S_t)$, features a contractionary state at time t, $S_t = RC_t$, and that RTS_t is true. Otherwise, if RTS_t is false, the contraction continues. The dating of deviation cycles is achieved by modifying this algorithm to account for the fact that a peak cannot occur if output is below trend, and a trough cannot occur if output is above it.

Artis *et al.* [21] also examine the properties of alternative filters such as the Hodrick–Prescott and Baxter–King filters for decomposing a time series into trend and cyclical components. They implement their procedures using data on euro area GDP and its components for the European Central Bank's (ECB) Area-Wide Model for the period 1970–2001.[4] Table 2.2 shows the business cycle turning points for both classical and deviation or growth cycles obtained using this approach. The Centre for Economic Policy Research (CEPR) has recently formed a committee to set the dates of the euro area business cycle. Its stated mission is to establish the chronology of recessions and expansions of the 11 original euro area member countries for 1970–1998 and of the current euro area as a whole since 1999. The turning points determined by the CEPR Business Cycle Dating Committee are also indicated in this table. We note that these are similar to the classical cycles identified by Artis *et al.* [21]. Finally,

Table 2.2.　　Euro Area Business Cycle Turning Points.

Peak	Trough
(1) Classical Cycles*	
1974 (III)	1975 (I)
1980 (I)	1981 (I)
1982 (II)	1982 (IV)
1992 (I)	1993 (I)
(2) Deviation Cycles*	
1974 (I)	1975 (III)
1976 (IV)	1977 (IV)
1980 (I)	1982 (IV)
1990 (II)	1993 (II)
1995 (I)	1997 (I)
1998 (I)	
(3) CEPR Dating Committee	
1974 (III)	1975 (I)
1980 (I)	1982 (IIII)
1992 (I)	1993 (III)

*Artis, Marcellino, and Proietti [21].

---

[4]See Fagan, Henry, and Mestre [85].

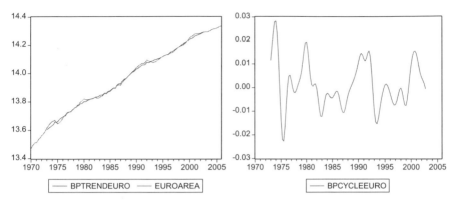

Fig. 2.3. Trend and Cyclical Components in Euro Area GDP.

Fig. 2.3 illustrates the logarithm of real GDP for the euro area and its trend and cyclical components estimated according to the Baxter–King filter for the period 1970(I)–2005(III).

Stock and Watson [199] provide a comprehensive analysis of the *volatility* and *persistence* of business cycles in G7 countries (defined to include the US, UK, France, Germany, Italy, Japan, and Canada) over the period 1960–2002. They find that the volatility of business cycles has moderated in most G7 countries over the past 40 years. They also provide evidence on the *synchronization* of international business cycles. They base their results on various measures of correlation of GDP growth across countries. First, they find no evidence for closer international synchronization over their period of study. This is similar to the findings of Köse, Prasad, and Terrones [139] and others. However, in sync with Artis *et al.* [20], they find evidence on the emergence of two cyclically coherent groups, the eurozone countries and English-speaking countries (including Canada, the UK, and the US).

Stock and Watson [199] also seek to provide evidence on the sources of the changes, namely, do they arise from changes in the magnitudes of the shocks or the nature of the propagation mechanism? Are the sources of the changes domestic or international? To answer these questions, they use a so-called factor-structural vector autoregression (FSVAR), which is specified in terms of the growth rates of quarterly GDP for the G7 countries. This is a standard structural vector autoregression (VAR) with an unobserved factor structure imposed on the VAR innovations. Let Y_t denote the $n \times 1$ vector of real GDP growth for the G7 countries considered in this study. The standard VAR model is given by

$$Y_t = A(L)Y_{t-1} + v_t, \tag{3.5}$$

where the vector of reduced-form errors v_t has the factor structure

$$v_t = \Gamma f_t + \epsilon_t, \tag{3.6}$$

where f_t is a $k \times 1$ vector with $k \leq n$. In this representation, the elements of ϵ_t denote the country-specific idiosyncratic shocks, and the elements of f_t denote the common international shocks. The covariance structure of the shocks is given by

$$E(f_t f_t') = diag(\sigma_{f1}, \ldots, \sigma_{fk})$$

and

$$E(v_t v_t') = diag(\sigma_{v1}, \ldots, \sigma_{vk}),$$

where the elements of f_t and ϵ_t are assumed to be mutually independent. Notice that the common shocks affect the output of multiple countries contemporaneously, whereas the idiosyncratic shocks affect them with a lag. This provides the identification scheme to help identify the common international shocks. The model allows for spillover effects to occur through the lagged effect of an idiosyncratic shock. These may arise from the role of international trade, for example.

Stock and Watson [199] find evidence for two common shocks. They also provide a variance decomposition for the impact of (i) the common international shocks, (ii) the domestic shocks, and (iii) the spillover effects of the domestic shocks on the h-step-ahead forecast error for each country. They consider two sample periods: 1960–1983 and 1984–2002. First, they find that most of the variance of GDP growth can be attributed to common and idiosyncratic domestic shocks. However, their relative variance varies by country and by time period. In the first period, the impact of international shocks is estimated to be greatest for countries such as Canada, France, and Germany, and the least for Italy and Japan. In the second period, domestic shocks explain almost all of the variance for Japan, reflecting the impact of the ten-year-long deflationary episode for this country. Second, the role of international sources of fluctuations arising from common shocks or from spillovers appears to have increased for the US, Canada, and Italy. However, they also show that the decline in overall volatility of GDP growth for countries such as the US, Germany, and the UK is due to the decline in the variance arising from international shocks. Their overall results indicate that the magnitudes of common international shocks appear to have become smaller in the 1980s and 1990s than they were in the 1960s and 1970s. This is the source of the moderation of individual business cycles, and also of the failure of business cycles to become more synchronized despite the great increase in trade flows over this period. Finally, they also find that shocks have become more persistent in countries such as Canada, France, and the UK.

2.4. IS THERE A WORLD BUSINESS CYCLE?

Köse, Otrok, and Whiteman [138] consider the issue of a *world* business cycle, and use data on 60-odd countries covering seven regions of the world to determine common factors underlying the cyclical fluctuations in the main macroeconomic aggregates (output, consumption, and investment) across all countries and regions as well as across countries and aggregates separately. They argue that many recent studies of international business cycles focus on a subset of countries — not the world.[5]

Their approach assumes that there are K unobservable factors that are hypothesized to characterize the dynamic interrelationship among a cross-country set of economic time series. Let N denote the number of countries, M the number of time series per country, and T the number of time periods. Let $y_{i,t}$ denote the observable variables for $i = 1, \ldots, N \times M$, $t = 1, \ldots, T$. There are three types of factors:

- N country-specific factors ($f_n^{country}$, one per each country);
- R regional factors (f_r^{region}, where r stands for North America, Latin America, Africa, Developed Asia, Developing Asia, Europe, or Oceania);
- the single world factor (f^{world}).

The behavior of each observable variable is related to the factors as follows:

$$y_{i,t} = a_i + b_i^{world} f_t^{world} + b_i^{region} f_{r,t}^{region} + b_i^{country} f_{n,t}^{country} + \epsilon_{i,t}, \qquad (4.7)$$

---

[5]For recent studies, see, for example, Gregory, Head, and Raynauld [109] or Lumsdaine and Prasad [154].

where $E(\epsilon_{i,t}\epsilon_{j,t}) = 0$ for $i \neq j$. The coefficients b_i^j denote the factor loadings, and show how much of the variation in $y_{i,t}$ can be explained by each factor. Thus, the model assumes that the behavior of $M \times N$ time series can be explained by $N + R + 1$ factors, where $N + R + 1 < MN$. Both the idiosyncratic errors and the factors are allowed to be serially correlated, and to follow autoregressions of orders p_i and q_k, respectively, as

$$\epsilon_{i,t} = \phi_{i,1}\epsilon_{i,t-1} + \phi_{i,2}\epsilon_{i,t-2} + \cdots + \phi_{i,p_i}\epsilon_{i,t-p_i} + u_{i,t}, \qquad (4.8)$$

where $E(u_{i,t}u_{i,t-s}) = \sigma_i^2$ for $i = j$ and $s = 0$, and zero otherwise. Let

$$f_{k,t} = \epsilon_{f_k,t}. \qquad (4.9)$$

Then,

$$\epsilon_{f_k,t} = \phi_{f_k,1}\epsilon_{f_k,t-1} + \phi_{f_k,2}\epsilon_{f_k,t-2} + \cdots + \phi_{f_k,q_k}\epsilon_{f_k,t-q_k} + u_{f_k,t}, \qquad (4.10)$$

where $E(u_{f_k,t}u_{f_k,t}) = \sigma_{f_k}^2$, $E(u_{f_k,t}u_{i,t-s}) = 0$ for all k, i, s. The innovations $u_{i,t}$, $i = 1, \ldots, M \times N$, and $u_{f_k,t}$, $k = 1, \ldots, K$, are mean zero, contemporaneously uncorrelated random variables. Thus, all the covariation among the observable series $y_{i,t}$ is due to the common factors, which themselves may be serially correlated.

Since the common factors are unobserved, we cannot identify uniquely the sign or scale of the factors or the factor loadings. One identification device is to assume that the factor loading on one of the factors is positive. For the world factor, the sign of the factor loading for US output is considered positive. Likewise, for the regional factor, the sign of the factor loading corresponding to North America is considered positive, and the country factors are identified by positive factor loadings on the output of each country. Finally, scales are identified by assuming that each $\sigma_{f_k}^2$ is equal to a constant. There are several ways to estimate this model. Since the factors are unobservable, one approach is to use a Kalman filtering algorithm together with classical statistical techniques to estimate the model's parameters; an alternative is to use Bayesian estimation techniques. This procedure yields a joint posterior distribution for the unobserved factors and the unknown parameters, conditional on the data. In what follows, we report results based on the median of the posterior distribution for the factors, and defer a discussion of the estimation techniques to Chapter 7.

Köse *et al.*'s paper [138] shows that the world factor identifies many of the major cyclical events over a 30-year period: the expansionary periods of the 1960s, the recession of the 1970s associated with the first oil shock, the recession of the 1980s associated with the debt crisis in developing countries and the tight monetary policies in the major developed countries, and the downturn and recession of the early 1990s. However, in contrast to models estimated using a smaller sample of countries, the world factor based on a large set of developed and developing countries implies that the recession of the 1980s was, if anything, *as* severe as the recession of the mid-1970s. Recall that the world, regional, and country factors are modeled as autoregressive processes which may display substantial persistence depending on the estimated values of the parameters. A second important finding from the paper is that most of the persistent co-movement across countries and aggregates is captured by the world factor. By contrast, the regional and country factors explain covariation or co-movement that is less persistent.

The paper also allows for a simple decomposition of variance attributed to the different factors. Using the representation of the model, we have that

$$Var(y_{i,t}) = (b_i^{world})^2 Var(f_t^{world}) + (b_i^{region})^2 Var(f_{r,t}^{region})$$
$$+ (b_i^{country})^2 Var(f_{n,t}^{country}) + Var(\epsilon_{i,t}). \qquad (4.11)$$

Thus, the fraction of variance attributed to the world factor can be expressed as

$$\frac{(b_i^{world})^2 Var(f_t^{world})}{Var(y_{i,t})}.$$

They find evidence that, first, the world factor explains nearly 15% of variation in output growth, 9% of consumption growth, and 7% of investment growth. They interpret this finding as evidence for a *world business cycle*. Second, the world factor is more successful in explaining economic activity in developed relative to developing countries. Third, country factors account for a much larger fraction of consumption growth than output growth. This finding has been documented further in the international business cycle literature, which is discussed in detail in Chapter 4.

The authors also document some noteworthy findings regarding the sources of volatility of investment growth. Specifically, they find that country and idiosyncratic factors account for a much larger share of variability in investment growth than the world and regional factors. Second, idiosyncratic shocks explain a much larger fraction of the volatility in investment growth in developing countries relative to developed countries. The authors pose this as a puzzle. However, much work on investment behavior shows that irreversible investment decisions are particularly susceptible to risk and uncertainty.[6] Altug, Demers, and Demers [10] argue that an important source of risk for developing countries is political risk or risk arising from the threat of expropriation, disruptions to market access, policy reversals, and debt and currency crises.[7] We conjecture that variability in investment due to such factors is a key channel for inducing idiosyncratic volatility in developing economies' investment behavior.

The last two findings of the paper imply that regional factors play a minor role in aggregate output fluctuations. Paralleling this finding, there is little evidence that the volatility of European aggregates can be attributed to the European regional factor. This last result is interpreted as evidence against the existence of a European business cycle. Yet this finding could also be due to model misspecification. As Stock and Watson [199] note, the dynamic factor model suffers from the shortcoming that all covariation is attributed to the common factors. Yet, there is also the possibility that some observed covariation could result from the spillover effects of idiosyncratic or country shocks, especially in an era of increased trade flows and financial integration.

2.5. HISTORICAL BUSINESS CYCLES

Basu and Taylor [31] examine business cycles within an international historical perspective. They consider the time series behavior of output, prices, real wages, exchange rates, total consumption, investment, and the current account for 15 countries including the US, the UK, and other European countries plus Argentina for the period since 1870. They divide this period into four periods that also reflect the monetary and capital account regimes prevailing in them.

- 1870–1941: This era corresponded to the classic gold standard. It featured fixed exchange rates and worldwide capital market integration.

---

[6] For recent reviews, see Caballero [53] or Demers, Demers, and Altug [79].

[7] In a related literature, Rodrik [178] emphasizes the importance of political risk (in his case, the risk of policy reversal) for irreversible investment decisions. Several studies document the importance of political risk in the unsuccessful recovery of private investment following the adoption of IMF stabilization packages in various countries. See, for example, Serven and Solimano [189].

- 1919–1939: During this period, the world economy shifted from a globalized regime to an autarkic regime. This period also corresponded to the Great Depression.
- 1945–1971: The third regime is the Bretton Woods era, which corresponded to the post-World War II era of reconstruction and a resumption of global trade and capital flows.
- Early 1970s–present: This period features a floating exchange regime and a period of increasing globalization.

Basu and Taylor [31] argue that considering such a breakdown allows for the analysis of the impact of different regimes on cyclical phenomena. It also provides a way to identify the importance of demand- versus supply-side factors or shocks and the role of alternative propagation mechanisms such as price rigidity. For example, most explanations of the Great Depression attribute the source of this massive downturn, which simultaneously occurred in a number of countries, to monetary phenomena. Consideration of alternative historical periods, including the era of the Great Depression, thus allows for an examination of such mechanisms as nominal rigidities in propagating shocks. Basu and Taylor [31] also argue that their periodization allows for an analysis of international capital flows and capital mobility in affecting cyclical fluctuations.

Bordo and Heibling [44] ask whether national business cycles have become more synchronized. They examine business cycles in 16 countries during the period 1880–2001, and consider the four exchange rate regimes also examined by Basu and Taylor [31]. The countries that they examine are Australia, Canada, Denmark, Finland, France, Germany, Italy, Japan, the Netherlands, Norway, Portugal, Spain, Sweden, Switzerland, the UK, and the US. Synchronization refers to the notion that "the timing and magnitudes of major changes in economic activity appear increasingly similar." Among other concepts, they use a statistical measure of synchronization developed by Harding and Pagan [115], the so-called concordance correlation, which examines whether the turning points in the different series occur at similar dates. Instead of using information on NBER-type reference dates, Bordo and Heibling [44] use real GDP or industrial production series to determine synchronization. They also use standard output correlations and factor-based measures.

To briefly describe the concordance correlations, let S_{it} and S_{jt} denote binary-cycle indicator variables which assume a value of 1 if the economy is in an expansion, 0 otherwise, for countries i and j. A simple measure of concordance is defined by the variable

$$I_{ij} = \frac{1}{T} \sum_{t=1}^{T} [S_{it} S_{jt} - (1 - S_{it})(1 - S_{jt})]. \tag{5.12}$$

Let $\bar{S}_i = (1/T) \sum_{t=1}^{T} S_{it}$ denote the estimated probability of being in an expansion, say; then under the assumption that S_{it} and S_{jt} are independent, the expected value of the concordance index is $2\bar{S}_i \bar{S}_j + 1 - \bar{S}_i - \bar{S}_j$. Subtracting this from I_{ij} yields the mean-corrected concordance index:

$$I_{ij}^* = 2\frac{1}{T} \sum_{t=1}^{T} (S_{it} - \bar{S}_i)(S_{jt} - \bar{S}_j). \tag{5.13}$$

To derive the concordance correlation coefficient, we divide I_{ij}^* by a consistent estimate of its standard error under the null hypothesis of independence. Note that the variance of I_{ij}^* is given by

$$Var(I_{ij}^*) = \frac{4}{T^2} E \left[\sum_{t=1}^{T} (S_{it} - \bar{S}_i)(S_{jt} - \bar{S}_j) \right].$$

If the two cycles are perfectly synchronized (so that $S_{it} = S_{jt}$ for all t), then the standardized index equals 1; if they are in different states in each period (so that $S_{it} = 1 - S_{jt}$), then the standardized index equals -1; and if the two cycles are unrelated, the standardized index equals 0.

Bordo and Heibling [44] calculate the business cycle indicators S_{it} for each of the four exchange rate regimes. They define a recession as one or more consecutive years of real GDP growth, while an expansion is defined as one or more years of positive GDP growth. They argue that $S_{it} = 1$ for most countries during the Bretton Woods era of 1948–1972 and hence leave this period out. For the gold standard era, they find that the average of the correlation coefficients is zero, as half of all pairs of business cycles are negatively related to each other while the other half are positively related. In the interwar and post-Bretton Woods era, more than half of all national business cycles become positively related to each other. The key finding is that during the classical gold standard, cycles were, on average, uncorrelated with each other; whereas beginning with the interwar period, they started becoming synchronized with each other. The authors also examine standard output correlations, which measure the magnitude as well as the direction of output changes. They find that there has been a tendency for higher, more positive bilateral output correlations by era. They also find higher output correlations for the core European countries (the EEC) and the Continental European countries. Finally, as in Stock and Watson [199], they find an increase in correlations for the Anglo-Saxon countries.

The authors also estimate a so-called static approximate factor model for the growth rates of GDP. In this model, there are no dynamics in the relation between output growth rates and the factors, and the idiosyncratic shocks are allowed to be serially correlated and heteroscedastic. They find that the variability of output due to variability in the common factors has "doubled from about 20 percent during the Gold Standard era to about 40 percent during the modern era of flexible exchange rates." They also estimate restricted versions of a FSVAR model along the lines of Stock and Watson [199] to determine the role of common shocks, idiosyncratic shocks, and spillover effects in generating this result. They consider a so-called *center country* version of this model, and a *trade linkages* version. In the former, lagged GDP growth of the center country is included alongside the lagged value of the own country's GDP growth in the VAR representation. In the trade linkages version, lagged GDP growth of the major trading partner is included in place of the center country's. They find that both global (common) shocks and transmission have become more important. However, the importance of transmission for peripheral countries arises only in the trade model, suggesting that it is not transmission from the center country that accounts for the increased role of transmission.

Bordo and Heibling [44] conclude by noting that global shocks are the dominant influence across all regimes, and that the increasing importance of global shocks reflects the forces of globalization, especially the integration of goods and services through international trade and the integration of financial markets. Eichengreen and Bordo [84] examine the nature of crises in two periods of globalization, before 1914 and after 1971. They argue that banking crises were less severe in the period before 1915, but this was not so for financial or twin crises. Typically, such crises have figured importantly in emerging market output fluctuations. We discuss emerging market business cycles in detail in Chapter 6.

Chapter 3

Models of Business Cycles

The standard approach to classifying business cycle models follows Ragnar Frisch's [95] terminology of impulses and propagation mechanisms. The shocks or impulses thought to instigate business cycles have typically been varied and diverse. Technology shocks which alter a society's production possibilities frontier, whether they are permanent or transitory such as oil shocks, have figured prominently in the recent literature. Weather shocks have always had a place among the impulses thought to trigger fluctuations in economic activity. Political shocks, wars, and other disruptions in market activity have also been acknowledged to play a role. More controversially, one could also assign a role to taste shocks or changes in preferences of consumers. Equivalently, one could argue, as Keynes [127] did, that investors' "animal spirits" or, more precisely, changes in their subjective beliefs could help to trigger business cycles.

Much of the controversy in the business cycle literature has stemmed from differences attached to the importance of alternative propagation mechanisms and the associated shocks. Current real business cycle (RBC) theory argues that business cycles can arise in frictionless, perfectly competitive, complete markets in which there are real or technology shocks. This approach emphasizes the role of *intertemporal substitution* motives in propagating shocks. By contrast, Keynesian and New Keynesian models stress the role of frictions such as *price stickiness*. In a simple labor market model, if real wages do not adjust downward when there is a negative shock to demand, the result is unemployment and greater declines in output relative to a situation with flexible prices. The Great

Depression and the recent financial crises also indicate the importance of *credit market frictions* and *financial accelerator-type effects* as a potential propagation mechanism for business cycles. In this case, shocks originating in various financial markets lead to a widening circle of bankruptcies and bank failures as well as large and negative effects on real output.[1]

In this chapter, we discuss variants of the RBC model. Since the debate has revolved around the efficacy of technology shocks and intertemporal substitution effects in replicating business cycles, it seems imperative to discuss the main propagation mechanisms of the RBC model. In the following chapter, we discuss an international RBC model to describe how the transmission mechanisms proposed by this approach translate into an open-economy setting.[2]

3.1. AN RBC MODEL

RBC theory has become popular in recent years because its micro foundations are fully specified and it links the short run with the neoclassical growth model. The prototypical RBC model has the structure of a standard neoclassical growth model with a labor/leisure choice incorporated. As Kydland and Prescott argue, this is a crucial modification as "more than half of business cycle fluctuations are accounted for by variations in the labor input" ([143], p. 173). There is a representative consumer who derives utility from consumption and leisure, and a constant-returns-to-scale (CRTS) production technology for producing the single good using labor and capital. All markets are perfectly competitive, all factors are fully employed, and all prices adjust instantaneously to clear markets. A number of these assumptions have come under criticism in the recent literature. The standard RBC model also assumes that there is no government, that households consume only goods produced in the market, and that there is no trade with the rest of the world. Some of the extensions of the RBC approach have modified the basic framework to incorporate the role of government, home production, and international trade. We will discuss these extensions in the following sections.

---

[1] See, for example, Bernanke and Gertler [40] or Kiyotaki and Moore [134].

[2] Rebelo [177] provides a recent review of alternative models and directions associated with the RBC agenda, but his discussion is abbreviated to satisfy the constraints imposed by a journal article.

Turning to the basic model, the representative agent has time-separable preferences over consumption and leisure choices given by

$$U = E_0 \left\{ \sum_{t=0}^{\infty} \beta^t u(c_t, l_t) \right\}, \tag{1.1}$$

where $0 < \beta < 1$ is the discount factor. For ease of exposition, we will suppose that the utility function has the form

$$U(c_t, l_t) = c_t^{\theta} l_t^{1-\theta}, \quad 0 < \theta < 1.$$

The time constraint requires that the sum of leisure and labor hours equals 1:

$$l_t + h_t = 1. \tag{1.2}$$

Hence, time spent not working is taken as leisure. There is a representative firm with CRTS production that is affected by a stochastic technology shock each period:

$$y_t = \exp{(z_t)} k_t^{\alpha} h_t^{1-\alpha}, \quad 0 < \alpha < 1. \tag{1.3}$$

Assume that the technology shock follows an AR(1) process:

$$z_{t+1} = \mu + \rho z_t + \epsilon_{t+1}, \quad 0 < \rho < 1, \ \epsilon_t \sim \text{i.i.d., and } N(0, \sigma_{\epsilon}^2). \tag{1.4}$$

Capital evolves according to

$$k_{t+1} = (1 - \delta)k_t + i_t, \tag{1.5}$$

where i_t denotes economy-wide investment and $0 < \delta < 1$ is the depreciation rate. The aggregate feasibility constraint is defined as

$$c_t + i_t = y_t. \tag{1.6}$$

Notice that the only shock in this model is the technology shock, which is assumed to be stationary but persistent as long as $\rho \neq 1$. We will discuss the propagation mechanism when describing the solution for the model.

The problem described above is an infinite-horizon dynamic stochastic optimization problem. The existence of a solution can be shown using standard recursive methods for analyzing such problems.[3] Assuming a solution exists,

---

[3] See, for example, Altug and Labadie [6] or Stokey and Lucas with Prescott [201].

let the value function associated with the problem be expressed as

$$V(k_t, z_t) = \max_{c_t, l_t, k_{t+1}} \{U(c_t, l_t) + \beta E_t V(k_{t+1}, z_{t+1})\} \qquad (1.7)$$

subject to

$$c_t + k_{t+1} = \exp(z_t) k_t^\alpha h_t^{1-\alpha} + (1-\delta)k_t,$$

$$l_t + h_t = 1.$$

Let λ_t denote the Lagrange multiplier on the resource constraint. Substituting for $l_t = 1 - h_t$ using the time constraint, the first-order conditions with respect to c_t, k_{t+1} and l_t and the envelope condition are

$$U_1(c_t, l_t) = \lambda_t, \qquad (1.8)$$

$$\beta E_t V_k(k_{t+1}, z_{t+1}) = \lambda_t, \qquad (1.9)$$

$$U_2(c_t, l_t) = \lambda_t \exp(z_t)(1-\alpha)k_t^\alpha h_t^{-\alpha}, \qquad (1.10)$$

$$V_k(k_t, z_t) = \lambda_t \left[\exp(z_t)\alpha k_t^{\alpha-1} h_t^{1-\alpha} + (1-\delta)\right], \qquad (1.11)$$

where U_{1t} and U_{2t} denote the marginal utility of consumption and leisure, respectively. These conditions can be rewritten as

$$\frac{U_{2t}}{U_{1t}} = \exp(z_t)(1-\alpha)(k_t/h_t)^\alpha \qquad (1.12)$$

$$\beta E_t \left\{ \frac{U_{1,t+1}}{U_{1t}} [\exp(z_{t+1})\alpha(k_{t+1}/h_{t+1})^{\alpha-1} + (1-\delta)] \right\} = 1. \qquad (1.13)$$

The first equation shows that the marginal rate of substitution between consumption and leisure is equal to the marginal product of labor. The second equation is the intertemporal Euler equation. Observe that the ratio U_2/U_1 is a function of the capital-labor ratio, k_t/h_t. There is no unemployment in the model as time not spent working is (optimally) taken as leisure. This means that the capital accumulation process will also be a function of the capital-labor ratio.

Suppose for the moment that there is no investment in the model, that is, $i_t = 0$, $k_t = \bar{k}$, and $c_t = y_t$. Notice that this is just a simple Robinson Crusoe economy in which the Crusoe produces output using capital and labor, which he then consumes. Thus, his choice is between how much to work and how much time to spend in leisure. To analyze the optimal consumption-leisure choice, we consider equation (1.12), which under our preference specification becomes

$$\frac{(1-\theta)c_t}{\theta l_t} = \exp(z_t)(1-\alpha)(k_t/h_t)^\alpha. \tag{1.14}$$

Substituting for $c_t = y_t = \exp(z_t)k_t^\alpha h_t^{1-\alpha}$ yields

$$\frac{(1-\theta)\exp(z_t)k_t^\alpha h_t^{1-\alpha}}{\theta(1-h_t)} = \exp(z_t)(1-\alpha)(k_t/h_t)^\alpha. \tag{1.15}$$

We can solve this equation for the optimal labor hours h_t^* as

$$h_t^* = \frac{\theta(1-\alpha)}{1-\theta+\theta\alpha}.$$

Thus, for example, if $\theta = 2/3$ and $\alpha = 1/2$, then Crusoe spends 50% of his time working and 50% taking leisure. Notice that the technology shock does not affect optimal hours worked because, for this preference specification, the income and substitution effects of an increase in productivity on hours worked cancel each other out. However, we note that if the substitution effect of an increase in productivity dominates the income effect, then Crusoe will work less in response to a temporary negative technology shock and will also consume and produce less. Figure 3.1 describes the representative agent's optimum.

Now suppose output can be consumed or invested so that $i_t \neq 0$. Then, in addition to equation (1.14), we have the intertemporal Euler equation characterizing the behavior of the optimal capital stock over time. Using our preference specification, we can rewrite the intertemporal Euler equation by noting that $U_1(c_{t+i}, l_{t+i}) = \theta(c_{t+i}/l_{t+i})^{\theta-1}$ for $i \geq 0$ and using the result in equation (1.14). This yields

$$\beta E_t \left\{ \left[\exp(z_{t+1}) \left(\frac{k_{t+1}}{h_{t+1}} \right)^\alpha \right]^{\theta-1} \left[\alpha \exp(z_{t+1}) \left(\frac{k_{t+1}}{h_{t+1}} \right)^{\alpha-1} + 1 - \delta \right] \right\}$$

$$= \left[\exp(z_t) \left(\frac{k_t}{h_t} \right)^\alpha \right]^{\theta-1}. \tag{1.16}$$

Now a temporary negative technology shock also affects investment or saving. Crusoe will typically respond to a temporary negative shock by lowering savings and also by working less. Thus, the impact of these changes is to induce fluctuations in labor supply and employment as well as investment.

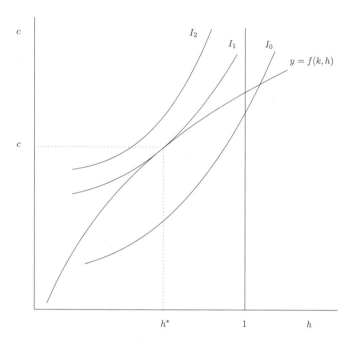

Fig. 3.1.   Robinson Crusoe's Optimum.

Furthermore, if the economy experiences a period with lower investment, it will have a lower capital stock in the future, implying that the effect of the shock persists.

We can also derive a measure of the Solow residual for this model by using the form of the production function. To derive the Solow residual, take the logarithm of both sides of equation (1.3) and then take the first differences:

$$\Delta \ln(y_{t+1}) = \Delta z_{t+1} + \alpha \Delta \ln(k_{t+1}) + (1 - \alpha)\Delta \ln(h_{t+1}).$$

To derive an observable measure of the Solow residual, the parameter α is typically measured as the share of capital in real output defined as $s_{kt} = r_t k_t / p_t y_t$, where r_t denotes the competitively determined rental rate on capital and p_t denotes the product price normalized here as unity. Under constant returns to scale, $s_{kt} + s_{ht} = 1$, where $s_{ht} = w_t h_t / p_t y_t$ denotes the share of labor in national income. Under these assumptions, the growth in the total factor productivity (TFP) is measured as a residual:

$$\Delta z_{t+1} = \Delta \ln(y_{t+1}) - s_{kt} \Delta \ln(k_{t+1}) - (1 - s_{kt})\Delta \ln(h_{t+1}).$$

Solow [196] showed that the residual accounted for about one half of the US GDP growth between 1909 and 1949. Similarly, according to Denison [80], 40% of GNP growth in the USA between 1929 and 1957 resulted from technical development. Notice that in the RBC framework the Solow residual is typically treated as *exogenous*. This is an issue that has been contested in the business cycle literature. Critics of the RBC approach argue that there are endogenous components to the fluctuations in the Solow residual, rendering the RBC interpretation invalid.

3.2. A NUMERICAL SOLUTION

We now provide a numerical solution to further illustrate the properties of the standard RBC model. We implement a quadratic approximation procedure that was initially suggested by Kydland and Prescott [141], and convert the original nonlinear dynamic optimization procedure to one which has a quadratic objective and linear constraints (see also Christiano [64]).

We assume that capital depreciates at the rate $0 < \delta < 1$ and the technology shock follows the process in (1.4). Since the utility function is strictly increasing, consumption plus investment equals output at the optimum. Using this fact, we can substitute for consumption in the utility function to obtain $u(c_t) = u(\exp{(z_t)}k_t^\alpha h_t^{1-\alpha} - i_t, 1 - h)$. Letting $u(c_t, 1 - h_t) = \theta \ln{(c_t)} + (1 - \theta)\ln{(1 - h_t)}, 0 < \theta < 1$, the problem now becomes

$$\max_{\{i_t, h_t\}_{t=0}^\infty} E_0 \left\{ \sum_{t=0}^\infty \left[\theta \ln{(\exp{(z_t)}k_t^\alpha h_t^{1-\alpha} - i_t)} + (1 - \theta)\ln{(1 - h_t)} \right] \right\}$$

subject to

$$k_{t+1} = (1 - \delta)k_t + i_t, \tag{2.17}$$

$$z_{t+1} = \mu + \rho z_t + \epsilon_{t+1}, \tag{2.18}$$

$$c_t \geq 0, \quad 0 \leq h_t \leq 1. \tag{2.19}$$

The quadratic approximation procedure is implemented as follows.

Step 1: Compute the deterministic steady state for the model. This is obtained by setting the exogenous technology shock equal to its mean value and evaluating the conditions (1.14) and (1.16) together with the feasibility conditions at constant values for c_t, k_t, and h_t. Let $\bar{z} = \mu/(1-\rho)$ denote the unconditional mean for the (log of) technology process. Using (1.16), we can solve for the steady-state capital-labor ratio as

$$\frac{\bar{k}}{\bar{h}} = \left(\alpha \frac{\exp(\bar{z})}{r+\delta}\right)^{1/(1-\alpha)}. \tag{2.20}$$

Next, note that in the deterministic steady state, investment is equal to depreciation:

$$\bar{i} = \delta\bar{k}. \tag{2.21}$$

Simplifying the result in (1.14), we obtain

$$\frac{1-\theta}{\theta} \frac{\bar{h}}{1-\bar{h}} = (1-\alpha)\frac{\bar{y}}{\bar{c}}, \tag{2.22}$$

where the aggregate feasibility constraint $\bar{c} + \delta\bar{k} = \bar{y} \equiv \exp\bar{z}\bar{k}^\alpha\bar{h}^{1-\alpha}$ is also assumed to hold. To find an explicit expression for $\bar{h}$ in terms of the underlying parameters, use the relation in (2.22) as

$$(1-\theta)\bar{h}\bar{c} = (1-\alpha)\theta(1-\bar{h})\bar{y}.$$

Rearranging, substituting for $\bar{c}$ first and then dividing through by $\bar{y}$, we obtain

$$(1-\theta)\bar{h}\left[1 - \delta\frac{\bar{k}}{\bar{y}}\right] + \theta(1-\alpha)\bar{h} = \theta(1-\alpha).$$

Now note that

$$\frac{\bar{k}}{\bar{y}} = \frac{\bar{k}}{\exp(\bar{z})\bar{k}^\alpha\bar{h}^{1-\alpha}} = \frac{(\bar{k}/\bar{h})^{1-\alpha}}{\exp(\bar{z})} = \frac{\alpha}{r+\delta}.$$

Substituting back into the equation defining $\bar{h}$ and simplifying yields

$$\bar{h}\left[(1-\theta) + \theta(1-\alpha) - (1-\theta)\delta\frac{\alpha}{r+\delta}\right] = \theta(1-\alpha),$$

or

$$\bar{h} = \frac{\theta(1-\alpha)(r+\delta)}{(r+\delta)(1-\theta\alpha) - (1-\theta)\delta\alpha}. \tag{2.23}$$

Step 2: Approximate the original utility function by a quadratic function around the deterministic steady state.[4] For this purpose, let $s \equiv (1, k, z, i, h)$ and $\bar{s} \equiv (0, \bar{z}, \bar{k}, \bar{i}, \bar{h})$. Approximate $u(s)$ near the deterministic steady state $\bar{s}$ using a second-order Taylor series approximation as

$$u(s) = u(\bar{s}) + (s - \bar{s})' \frac{\partial u(s)}{\partial s} + \frac{1}{2}(s - \bar{s})' \frac{\partial^2 u(s)}{\partial s \partial s'}(s - \bar{s}).$$

Define e as the 5×1 vector with a 1 in the first row and zeros elsewhere. Notice that the utility function can be written as

$$u(s) = (s - \bar{s})' T (s - \bar{s}),$$

where

$$T = e \left[u(\bar{s}) + \frac{1}{2} \bar{s}' \frac{\partial^2 u(s)}{\partial s \partial s'} \bar{s} \right] e'$$

$$+ \frac{1}{2} \left(\frac{\partial u(s)}{\partial s} e' + e \frac{\partial u(s)'}{\partial s} \right) + \frac{1}{2} \left(\frac{\partial^2 u(s)}{\partial s \partial s'} \right),$$

where all partial derivatives are evaluated at $\bar{s}$.

Define the vector of state variables as $x_t = (1, k_t - \bar{k}, z_t - \bar{z})'$ and the vector of control variables as $u_t = (i_t - \bar{i}, h_t - \bar{h})'$. We can write the law of motion for the state variables as

$$\begin{bmatrix} 1 \\ k_{t+1} \\ z_{t+1} \end{bmatrix} = \begin{bmatrix} 1 & 0 & 0 \\ 0 & (1-\delta) & 0 \\ \mu & 0 & \rho \end{bmatrix} \begin{bmatrix} 1 \\ k_t \\ z_t \end{bmatrix} + \begin{bmatrix} 0 & 0 & 0 \\ 0 & 1 & 0 \\ 0 & 0 & 0 \end{bmatrix} \begin{bmatrix} 0 \\ i_t \\ 0 \end{bmatrix} + \begin{bmatrix} 0 \\ 0 \\ \epsilon_{t+1} \end{bmatrix}.$$

Notice that $s - \bar{s} = (x, u)'$. Thus, the quadratic form $(s - \bar{s})' T (s - \bar{s})$ can be written as

$$(s - \bar{s})' T (s - \bar{s}) = \begin{bmatrix} x \\ u \end{bmatrix}' \begin{bmatrix} T_{11} & T_{12} \\ T_{21} & T_{22} \end{bmatrix} \begin{bmatrix} x \\ u \end{bmatrix}$$

$$= \begin{bmatrix} x \\ u \end{bmatrix}' \begin{bmatrix} R & W \\ W' & Q \end{bmatrix} \begin{bmatrix} x \\ u \end{bmatrix}.$$

---

[4] An alternative approach is to log-linearize the model. See Campbell [55].

Step 3: Convert the original dynamic optimization problem into a problem with linear constraints and a quadratic objective function. Using the definition of T, x_t, and u_t, the dynamic optimization problem can now be written as

$$\max_{\{u_t\}_{t=0}^{\infty}} E_0 \left\{ \sum_{t=0}^{\infty} \beta^t [x_t' R x_t + u_t' Q u_t + 2x_t' W u_t] \right\} \qquad (2.24)$$

subject to the linear law of motion

$$x_{t+1} = Ax_t + Bu_t + \varepsilon_{t+1}, \quad t \geq 0, \qquad (2.25)$$

where $E(\varepsilon_{t+1}) = 0$ and $E(\varepsilon_t \varepsilon_t') = \Sigma$. This is now an optimal control problem with a quadratic objective and linear constraints. Such problems can be solved using the methods for solving dynamic optimization problems that satisfy a certainty equivalence property; in other words, the solution for the stochastic optimal control problem is identical to the solution for the deterministic version of the problem with the shocks ε_{t+1} replaced by their expectation $E(\varepsilon_{t+1})$. This class of problems is known as *optimal linear regulator problems*. Ljungqvist and Sargent [146] and Anderson, Hansen, McGrattan, and Sargent [16] provide further discussion of the formulation and estimation of linear dynamic economic models.

Bellman's equation for this problem is given by

$$V(x_t) = \max_{u_t} \left\{ x_t' R x_t + u_t' Q u_t + 2u_t' W x_t + \beta E[V(x_{t+1})] \right\}$$

subject to $x_{t+1} = Ax_t + Bu_t + \varepsilon_{t+1}$. Given the structure of the problem, notice that the value function will be a quadratic function in the state variables:

$$V(x) = x' P x + d,$$

where d and P are quantities to be determined. Substituting for next period's state variables and using this expression for the value function, Bellman's equation becomes

$$x' P x + d = \max_u \left\{ x' R x + u' Q u + 2x' W u \right.$$

$$\left. + \beta E \left[(Ax + Bu + \varepsilon)' P(Ax + Bu + \varepsilon) + d \right] \right\}. \qquad (2.26)$$

The first-order conditions with respect to u are

$$Qu + W'x + \beta[B'PAx + B'PBu] = 0.^5 \tag{2.27}$$

Solving for u yields

$$u = -(Q + \beta B'PB)^{-1}(W'x + \beta B'PAx) = -Fx, \tag{2.28}$$

where

$$F = (Q + \beta B'PB)^{-1}(\beta B'PA + W'). \tag{2.29}$$

Notice that the shocks ε_{t+1} do not affect the optimal choice of u_t. Substituting for u back into the definition of $V(x)$ yields

$$P = R + \beta A'PA - (\beta A'PB + W)(Q + \beta B'PB)^{-1}(\beta B'PA + W'),$$
$$d = (1 - \beta)^{-1}[\beta E(\varepsilon' P\varepsilon)].$$

The equation for P is known as the *algebraic matrix Riccati* equation for so-called optimal linear regulator problems.[6] The solution for P can be obtained by iterating on the matrix Riccati difference equation:

$$P_{n+1} = R + \beta A'P_nA - (\beta A'P_nB + W)(Q + \beta B'P_nB)^{-1}(\beta B'P_nA + W'),$$

starting from $P_0 - 0$. The policy function associated with P_n is

$$F_{n+1} = (Q + \beta B'P_nB)^{-1}(\beta B'P_nA + W').$$

In the RBC literature, the model is then calibrated with the data. Calibration refers to the practice of determining the parameters of the model based on its steady state properties and the results of other studies, given particular functional forms for the production function and the utility function (see Cooley and Prescott [75]). A stochastic process for z_t is also specified and a random number generator is used to simulate the TFP time series. The simulated series are used to generate time series for consumption, output,

---

[5]To derive this result, we have used the rules for differentiating quadratic forms as

$$\frac{\partial u'Qu}{\partial u} = [Q + Q']u = 2Qu, \quad \frac{\partial x'Tu}{\partial u} = T'x \text{ and } \frac{\partial u'Tx}{\partial u} = Tx.$$

[6]Notice that the matrices R, Q, A, and B must be further restricted to ensure the existence of a solution to the matrix difference equation defining P_n. One condition that suffices is that the eigenvalues of A are bounded in modulus below unity.

investment, and labor. Trends in the data are removed using a given filter. The means, variances, covariances, and cross-correlations for the simulated time series are compared to the comparable statistics in the data. The model is then judged to be close or not close based on this comparison, so the approach differs significantly from standard econometrics.

We now illustrate this solution method for the standard RBC model with a labor-leisure choice presented at the beginning of this section. Consider the parameter values $\beta = 0.95$, $\alpha = 1/3$, $\theta = 0.36$, $\delta = 0.10$, $\rho = 0.95$, and $\sigma = 0.028$. The steady values for the variables are given by $\bar{k} = 1.1281$, $\bar{i} = 0.1128$, $\bar{y} = 0.4783$, $\bar{c} = 0.3655$, and $\bar{h} = 0.2952$. We first calculate a set of unconditional moments that have been used in the RBC literature to match the model with the data. These are obtained by simulating the behavior of the different series across a given history of the shock sequence. Specifically, we draw a sequence of shocks $\{\hat{\epsilon}_{t+1}\}_{t=0}^{2999}$ that are normally distributed with mean zero and standard deviation 0.028, and generate a sequence of technology shocks beginning from some initial value z_0 as $\hat{z}_{t+1} = \rho z_t + \hat{\epsilon}_{t+1}$. We then use the linear decision rules for all variables to simulate for the endogenous variables based on the same history of shocks. Finally, we calculate unconditional moments for the different series after dropping the first 1000 observations.

The typical set of unconditional moments used in the RBC literature is displayed in Table 3.1. We find that consumption fluctuates slightly less than output and investment fluctuates significantly more. Likewise, productivity is almost as variable as output. By contrast, we find that the variation in hours is typically quite low. In terms of the correlation of each series with output, we find that all series are procyclical, with hours showing the least procyclicality. The RBC theorists have interpreted these results as implying that, in the first instance, the model is capable of delivering some of the salient features

Table 3.1. Cyclical Properties of Key Variables.

	Standard Deviation (%)	Correlation with Output
Output	8.8616	1
Consumption	8.1134	0.9163
Investment	12.9238	0.9807
Hours	1.6684	0.4934
Productivity	7.7496	0.9840

of the data. Specifically, the model predicts that consumption fluctuates less than output whereas investment fluctuates more, as we observe in the data. Consumption, investment, and productivity are all strongly procyclical. In terms of the variation accounted by the technology shocks, the technology shock explains much but not all of the variation in output. Thus, the RBC model has been viewed as being able to generate cycles endogenously and having economic significance even if the calibration method is controversial. This is discussed further in the following sections.

Figure 3.2 illustrates the response of all the variables to a 1% shock in technology starting from the steady-state capital stock. We note that hours and output both increase and then fall back to a lower level. The percentage change in output exceeds the percentage change in the technology shock because optimal hours also show a positive response to the technology shock. By contrast, capital and consumption show a humped-shaped response, rising first and then declining back to a lower level. Consumption shows a gradual positive response because investment is initially high. These responses have been widely

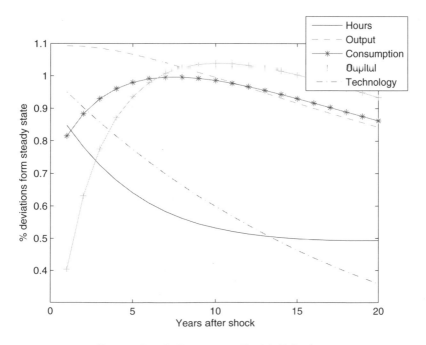

Fig. 3.2.   Impulse Responses to a Shock in Technology.

documented in the RBC literature (see, for example, Uhlig [206]). The positive response of hours to a positive productivity shock has also become an important point of difference between models that assume perfectly flexible prices versus those that assume nominal price rigidity. We discuss New Keynesian models with monopolistic competition and prices that are fixed in the short run in Chapter 5.

3.3. INITIAL CRITICISMS

In perhaps what is the most famous example of an RBC model, Kydland and Prescott [141] formulated a real business cycle model in which preferences are not separable over time with respect to leisure and there exists a time-to-build feature in investment for new capital goods. The production function displays constant returns to scale with respect to hours worked and a composite capital good. The only exogenous shock to their model is a random technology shock which follows a stationary first-order autoregressive process. They use the quadratic approximation procedure to obtain linear decision rules for a set of aggregate variables, and generate time series for the remaining series by drawing realizations of the innovation to the technology shock. They calculate a small set of moments associated with each series to match the model with the data.

When calibrating their model, Kydland and Prescott choose the variance of the innovation to the technology shock to make the variability of the output series generated by their model equal to the variability of observed GNP. As McCallum [156] notes, this feature of their analysis makes it difficult to judge whether "technology shocks are adequate to generate output, employment, etc. fluctuations of the magnitude actually observed." One of the most pervasive criticisms of the model is that there is no evidence of large, economy-wide disturbances that can play the role of the technology shocks posited by Kydland and Prescott. The only exception is oil price shocks, leading one to question whether the model was developed in reaction to the supply-side disturbances that characterized the 1970s. The RBC approach in general has difficulty in answering what some other examples of big shocks are. Summers [202] argues that "the vast majority of what Prescott labels technology shocks are in fact observable concomitants of labor hoarding and other behavior which Prescott does not allow for in his model." This point was subsequently elaborated on by Hall [110, 111], who argued that the procyclical movements in the Solow residual were, in fact, endogenous changes in efficiency arising from labor hoarding, increasing returns to scale, or price markups.

Summers [202] also took issue with the parameters of the model that Kydland and Prescott [141] or Prescott [173] advocated in their calibration exercise. He argued that the econometric evidence presented by Eichenbaum, Hansen, and Singleton [83] on the intertemporal substitution of leisure hypothesis pointed to a share of time allocated to market activities that was more in the range of one-sixth, not one-third. He also noted that a real interest rate of 4% was inconsistent with the historical evidence of very low yields averaging around 1%. Singleton [192] raised the problem of inference and sampling uncertainty surrounding the various measures of fit proposed in the RBC literature. He noted that the calibration approach did not provide a straightforward and transparent way of judging whether a given model constituted an improvement over another model. Eichenbaum [82] raised the issue of the model's fit based on the ratio of variance for GDP implied by the model and the data. Eichenbaum showed that the standard error of this ratio was heavily influenced by the parameters of the assumed stochastic process for the technology shock.

The policy implications of the RBC model have also come under attack. According to the RBC model, business cycle fluctuations are Pareto optimal and there is no role for the government to try to smooth or mitigate the fluctuations. In fact, such policy efforts are inefficient. Prescott [173] commented as follows:

> Economic theory predicts that, given the nature of the shocks to technology and people's willingness and ability to intertemporally and intratemporally substitute, the economy will display fluctuations like those the U.S. economy displays. . . . Indeed, if the economy did not display the business cycle phenomena, there would be a puzzle.

Thus, according to this approach, cyclical fluctuations are viewed as the natural response of the economy to changes that affect individuals' consumption or production decisions. However, if prices or wages are fixed or rigid or if there are other types of frictions arising from credit markets, then the policy implications of the RBC approach may not be valid and the economy may operate with high levels of unemployment and excess capacity over long periods. In this case, government policies may be required to move the economy towards a full employment level.

In the chapters that follow, we will discuss the efficacy of the RBC model in serving as a model of aggregate fluctuations as well as questions that have lingered to this day about the adequacy of the calibration approach in matching the model to the data.

3.4. "PUZZLES"

Many of the initial criticisms which had been voiced by opponents of the RBC approach took on the character of "puzzles". These puzzles have constituted the basis of much further research in the area.

We can list some of these puzzles as follows:

- **The variability of hours and productivity**: As seen in Table 3.1, one of the main problems with the standard RBC model is that it cannot capture the variation in the aggregate labor input (see also Kydland [140]). In the data, employment is strongly procyclical and almost as variable as output while real wages are weakly procyclical. In the standard model, a productivity shock shifts the marginal product of labor so that the observed variations in employment can only occur if the labor supply curve is relatively elastic. Yet, micro studies find that wage elasticity of labor supply is quite low. In this case, the marginal productivity shock should lead to most of the adjustment in real wages and less in the quantity of labor. Furthermore, in the data, hours of work per worker adjusts very little over the cycle. About two-thirds of the variability in total hours worked comes from movements into and out of the labor force, and the rest is due to adjustment in the number of hours worked per employee. These findings create a puzzle for the standard RBC model.

- **The productivity puzzle**: In the data, the correlation between productivity and hours worked is near zero or negative, while the correlation between productivity and output is positive and around 0.5.[7] By contrast, the RBC model, which is driven entirely by productivity shocks, generates correlations that are large and positive in both cases. Another problem that

---

[7] See, for example, Christiano and Eichenbaum [65], who measure hours worked and productivity based on both household and establishment-level surveys conducted by the US Department of Labor.

arises in matching the model and the data is that in the data, labor's share of income moves countercyclically, whereas in the RBC model labor's share is fixed.

- **Reverse causality**: The stylized facts of business cycles state that money, especially M2, appears to be a leading indicator of aggregate output. However, this is inconsistent with the notion that TFP shocks are the driving force behind business cycle activity. The conventional wisdom regarding the money-output correlation, summarized by Friedman and Schwartz [94] in their study of monetary history, is that the causality goes from money to output but with "long and variable lags".

3.4.1. *A Model with Indivisible Labor Supply*

The indivisible labor, lottery models studied by Gary Hansen [112] and Richard Rogerson [179] have been used to explain the stylized fact that aggregate hours vary more than productivity does. This framework also provides a way for reconciling large labor supply elasticities at the aggregate level with low labor supply elasticities at the individual level. This is accomplished by assuming that individuals can work all the time or not at all. To account for the nonconvexities introduced by the work/nonwork decision, it is assumed that individuals choose the probability of working, π_t. A lottery then determines whether an individual actually works. This economy is one in which individuals and a firm trade a contract that commits the household to work h_0 hours with probability π_t. Since what is being traded is the contract, the individual gets paid regardless of whether he works or not. We now describe a version of the RBC model due to Rogerson [179] and Hansen [112] that allows for fixed costs and nonconvexities in labor supply.

Suppose that workers are constrained to work either zero or $\hat{h}$ hours, where

$$0 < \hat{h} < 1. \tag{4.30}$$

The main idea is that there are nonconvexities or fixed costs that make varying the number of employed workers more efficient than varying hours per worker. Let π_t denote the probability that a given agent is employed in period t so that the number of per capita hours worked is given by

$$H_t = \pi_t \hat{h}. \tag{4.31}$$

Let $c_{0,t}$ denote the consumption of an unemployed worker and $c_{1,t}$ denote the consumption of an employed agent. Then the expected utility of the representative consumer, taking into account the work versus nonwork decision, is given by

$$E[u(c_t, l_t)] = \pi_t u(c_{1,t}, 1 - \hat{h}) + (1 - \pi_t)u(c_{0,t}, 1).$$

Assume that the individual utility function has the form

$$u(c, l) = \ln(c) + A\ln(l). \tag{4.32}$$

The social planner solves the problem

$$\max_{\pi_t, c_{0,t}, c_{1,t}} E[u(c_t, l_t)] \text{ s.t. } \pi_t c_{1,t} + (1 - \pi_t)c_{0,t} = c_t.$$

Notice that the social planner chooses the consumption allocations of each agent plus the probability of their working. When agents do work, they must supply $\hat{h}$ hours of work so that there is no choice over hours of work directly. Let λ_t denote the Lagrange multiplier on the feasibility constraint for consumption. Omitting the work/leisure decision for the moment, the first-order conditions with respect to $(c_{0,t}, c_{1,t})$ are

$$\frac{1 - \pi_t}{c_{0,t}} = (1 - \pi_t)\lambda_t, \tag{4.33}$$

$$\frac{\pi_t}{c_{1,t}} = \pi_t \lambda_t. \tag{4.34}$$

It follows that $c_{0,t} = c_{1,t} = c_t$ so that the agent consumes the same amount whether or not he is working. Hence, the unemployed worker enjoys higher utility since working causes disutility. In this model, *ex ante* all individuals are alike, but *ex post* they differ because some work while others enjoy leisure. With complete insurance and identical preferences that are separable with respect to consumption and leisure, all individuals have the same consumption but the unemployed are better off. This is a feature that is counterfactual to the working of actual labor markets.

Notice that the agent will consume c_t whether or not he is working. Hence, expected utility (where the expectation is over whether or not you work) is

$$\ln(c_t) + \pi_t A\ln(1 - \hat{h}) + (1 - \pi_t)A\ln(1), \tag{4.35}$$

where A is a positive constant. Using the definition of H_t, $\pi_t = H_t/\hat{h}$. Now substitute for π_t in (4.35) and use $\ln(1) = 0$ to obtain

$$E[u(c_t, l_t)] = \ln(c_t) + \pi_t A \ln(1 - \hat{h})$$

$$= \ln(c_t) - BH_t, \tag{4.36}$$

where

$$B = \frac{-A \ln(1 - \hat{h})}{\hat{h}}.$$

Comparing equation (4.32) with equation (4.36) shows the effect of the lottery assumption. The former specification for preferences implies a low intertemporal elasticity of substitution in labor supply, which is consistent with assumptions about individual behavior. By contrast, the latter specification — which is linear in total hours H_t — implies a high intertemporal elasticity at the aggregate level.

The preferences can now be written as

$$U = E_0 \left\{ \sum_{t=0}^{\infty} \beta^t u(c_t, H_t) \right\},$$

where $u(c_t, H_t) = \ln(c_t) - BH_t$. We now solve the model subject to the time constraint, resource constraint, production function, and law of motion for the capital stock described earlier. The problem is

$$\max_{\{c_t, H_t, k_{t+1}\}} E_0 \left\{ \sum_{t=0}^{\infty} \beta^t \left[\ln(c_t) - BH_t + \lambda_t [\exp(z_t) k_t^{\theta} H_t^{1-\theta} \right. \right.$$

$$\left. \left. + (1 - \delta) k_t - c_t - k_{t+1}] \right] \right\}.$$

The first-order conditions are

$$\frac{1}{c_t} = \lambda_t, \tag{4.37}$$

$$B = \lambda_t \exp(z_t)(1 - \theta) k_t^{\theta} H_t^{-\theta}, \tag{4.38}$$

$$\lambda_t = \beta E_t \lambda_{t+1} \left[\exp(z_{t+1}) \theta k_{t+1}^{\theta-1} H_{t+1}^{1-\theta} + (1 - \delta) \right]. \tag{4.39}$$

Notice that (4.38) can be used to solve for H_t as

$$H_t = \left(\frac{Bc_t}{\exp{(z_t)}(1-\theta)}\right)^{-1/\theta} k_t$$

$$= \left(-\frac{A\ln{(1-\hat{h})}c_t}{\exp{(z_t)}(1-\theta)\hat{h}}\right)^{-1/\theta} k_t. \qquad (4.40)$$

Equations (4.37) and (4.39) yield the intertemporal Euler equation as

$$1 = \beta\left\{\frac{c_t}{c_{t+1}}[\exp{(z_{t+1})}\theta k_{t+1}^{\theta-1}H_{t+1}^{1-\theta} + (1-\delta)]\right\}, \qquad (4.41)$$

where the term in square brackets shows the rate of return to investing in the aggregate production technology. With H_t determined in (4.40), we can use the resource constraint to solve for c_t and then substitute for c_t into the intertemporal Euler equation to obtain a nonlinear stochastic in k_{t+1} with forcing process $\{z_t\}$.

Hansen [112] calibrates this model by specifying values for the unknown parameters θ, δ, β, A, and the stochastic process for the technology shock using the approach in Kydland and Prescott [141]. Hansen argues that the model with indivisibilities can generate a variability of hours relative to productivity around 2.7 compared to the model without indivisibilities which implies a value near unity. The purpose of the framework that Hansen [112] and Rogerson [179] consider is to generate the stylized fact with respect to the relative variability of hours versus productivity, and it is not intended to incorporate the microeconomic foundations of the labor market.[8]

3.4.2. *The Productivity Puzzle*

Several resolutions of the productivity puzzle have been suggested. These typically specify an extra margin regarding individuals' choices that helps break the close link between hours and productivity implied by the standard model.

---

[8]See Browning, Hansen, and Heckman [48] for further discussion regarding the reconciliation of micro evidence with dynamic general equilibrium models.

Government Consumption Shocks

Christiano and Eichenbaum [65] note that as long as there is a single shock that drives the behavior of both hours and productivity, the standard model cannot deliver the strong procyclical response of hours without procyclical behavior in productivity. They generate the negative correlation between hours worked and real wages or productivity by introducing government consumption shocks.

They consider a prototypical RBC model with a labor/leisure choice, and utilize the solution of the social planner's problem to derive the competitive equilibrium allocations. Let $\bar{N}$ denote the time endowment of the representative household per period. The social planner ranks alternative consumption/leisure streams according to

$$E_0 \left\{ \sum_{t=0}^{\infty} \beta^t [\ln (c_t) + \gamma V(\bar{N} - n_t)] \right\}, \tag{4.42}$$

where c_t denotes consumption and $\bar{N} - n_t$ denotes leisure of the representative household. Consumption services c_t are related to private and public consumption as follows:

$$c_t = c_t^p + \alpha g_t, \tag{4.43}$$

where c_t^p is private consumption, g_t is public consumption, and α is a parameter that governs the impact of government consumption on the marginal utility of private consumption. They consider two different specifications for the labor/leisure choice, one which is based on a time-separable logarithmic specification and a second which incorporates the Hansen indivisible labor assumption, namely,

$$V(\bar{N} - n_t) = \begin{cases} \ln (\bar{N} - n_t) \\ \bar{N} - n_t \end{cases} \tag{4.44}$$

for all t. Per capita output is produced according to the Cobb–Douglas production function

$$y_t = (z_t n_t)^{1-\theta} k_t^{\theta}, \quad 0 < \theta < 1, \tag{4.45}$$

where z_t is a technology shock which evolves according to the process

$$z_t = z_{t-1} \exp (\lambda_t). \tag{4.46}$$

In this equation, λ_t is an independent and identically distributed process with mean λ and standard deviation σ_λ. The aggregate resource constraint stipulates that consumption plus investment cannot exceed output in each period:

$$c_t^p + g_t + k_{t+1} - (1 - \delta)k_t \le y_t. \tag{4.47}$$

Since the technology shock follows a logarithmic random walk, the solution for the model can be more fruitfully expressed in terms of the transformed variables $\bar{k}_{t+1} = k_{t+1}/z_t$, $\bar{y}_t = y_t/z_t$, $\bar{c}_t = c_t/z_t$, and $\bar{g}_t = g_t/z_t$. The specification of the model is completed by assuming a stochastic law of motion for $\bar{g}_t$ as

$$\ln(\bar{g}_t) = (1 - \rho)\ln(\bar{g}) + \rho\ln(\bar{g}_{t-1}) + \mu_t, \tag{4.48}$$

where $\ln(\bar{g})$ is the mean of $\ln(\bar{g}_t)$, $|\rho| < 1$, and μ_t is the innovation to $\ln(\bar{g}_t)$ with standard deviation σ_μ.

In this model, government consumption shocks lead to shifts in the labor supply curve so that, in the absence of technology shocks, hours of work can increase along a downward-sloping labor demand curve. The key assumption is that private and government consumption are not perfect substitutes. Hence, an increase in government consumption leads to a negative wealth effect for consumers through the economy-wide resource constraint. If leisure is a normal good, hours increase and average productivity declines in response to a positive government consumption shock.

Home Production

Another way of improving the model's ability to match the data is to introduce home production. Following Benhabib, Rogerson, and Wright [39], consider a decision-maker who has preferences

$$\sum_{t=0}^{\infty} \beta^t u(c_{mt}, c_{ht}, h_{mt}, h_{ht}),$$

where $0 < \beta < 1$. In this expression, c_{mt} is the consumption of a market good; c_{ht} is consumption of the home-produced good; h_{mt} is labor time spent in market work; and h_{ht} is labor time spent in home work. Assume that $u_1 > 0$, $u_2 > 0$, $u_3 < 0$, and $u_4 < 0$. The total amount of time available to the household is normalized as unity, and leisure is defined as time not spent working in the market or at home:

$$l_t = 1 - h_{mt} - h_{ht}.$$

At each date, the household can purchase market goods c_{mt}, market capital goods k_{mt}, and household capital goods k_{ht}. Household capital goods are used in home production, but market capital goods are rented to firms at the competitive rental rate r_t. Letting w_t denote the wage rate and δ_m and δ_h denote the depreciation rates on market and home capital, respectively, the household's budget constraint is

$$c_{mt} + k_{m,t+1} + k_{h,t+1} \leq w_t h_{mt} + r_t k_{mt} + (1 - \delta_m) k_{mt} + (1 - \delta_h) k_{ht}.$$

Home goods are produced according to the home production function:

$$c_{ht} = g(h_{ht}, k_{ht}, z_{ht}),$$

where z_{ht} is a shock to home production and g is increasing and concave in labor and capital.

Alternative measures put home production to be in the range of 20–50% of GDP. In the model, home production is used to produce a nontradeable consumption good. A rise in market productivity may induce households to substitute away from home production towards market production. This gives us another margin to substitute market labor and improves the model's predictions. Unlike the standard model, the labor supply curve also shifts in response to a good productivity shock, thereby leading to greater variability in labor. However, one criticism of the home production theory is that it suggests that all movements out of the labor force (toward home production) are **voluntary**.

Labor Hoarding

A third way to resolve the productivity puzzle is through a labor hoarding argument. This says that the effective labor input can be altered even though the total number of workers is fixed. The firm may not alter its work force every time there is a productivity shock (which would occur through a shift in the marginal product of labor curve). However, if there are costs to hiring or laying workers off, then firms may retain workers even though they are not exerting much effort. Hence, labor effort is likely to be adjusted first in response to a productivity shock. Eventually more workers may be hired or fired, but only after longer periods of time.

To illustrate the role of labor hoarding, consider a production function for aggregate output Y_t which depends on an exogenous technology shock A_t, capital K_t, and a labor input that reflects variations in work effort following Burnside, Eichenbaum, and Rebelo [52]. Specifically, let f denote a fixed shift length; N_t, the total number of workers; and W_t, the work effort of each individual. Thus,

$$Y_t = A_t K_t^\alpha [f N_t W_t]^{1-\alpha}, \quad 0 < \alpha < 1.$$

In the standard model, the production function can be written as

$$Y_t = S_t K_t^\alpha [H_t]^{1-\alpha},$$

where H_t denotes the total hours worked. In the absence of variations in work effort, $H_t = f N_t$. Notice that the conventionally measured Solow residual S_t is related to true technology shock A_t as

$$\ln(S_t) = \ln(A_t) + \alpha \ln(K_t) + (1-\alpha)[\ln(f) + \ln(N_t) + \ln(W_t)]$$
$$- \alpha \ln(K_t) - (1-\alpha)[\ln(f) + \ln(N_t)]$$
$$= \ln(A_t) + (1-\alpha)\ln(W_t).$$

Decisions to alter effort levels will be the outcome of a maximizing decision, so that the movements in the Solow residual are not entirely exogenous. If labor hoarding is included in the model, then the productivity/hours correlation is reduced and more closely matches the data. The comments made regarding fluctuations in the effort level of labor also apply to capital. The measured capital in the Solow residual does not take into account optimal fluctuations in capital utilization rates. This can lead to variation in the Solow residual that is not related to changes in productivity or technology.

3.4.3. *Reverse Causality*

One approach to dealing with this criticism is to introduce money and banking into the standard RBC model following King and Plosser [129]. These authors observe that transactions services (as provided by money and the banking sector) can be viewed as an intermediate input that reduces the cost of producing output and, hence, can be treated as a direct input into the aggregate production function. To briefly describe their framework, suppose the final good is produced according to the production technology

$$y_t = f(k_{ft}, n_{ft}, d_{ft})\phi_t, \tag{4.49}$$

where k_{ft} is the amount of capital, n_{ft} is the amount of labor services, and d_{ft} is the amount of transactions services used in the final goods industry. In this expression, ϕ_t is a shock to production of the final good at time t. The financial industry is assumed to provide accounting services that facilitate the exchange of goods by reducing the amount of time that would be devoted to market transactions. The production of the intermediate good is given by

$$d_t = g(n_{dt}, k_{dt})\lambda_t, \tag{4.50}$$

where n_{dt} and k_{dt} denote the amounts of labor and capital allocated to the financial sector, respectively, and λ_t captures technological innovations to the financial services industry. Households maximize the expected discounted value of utility from consumption c_t and leisure l_t as

$$E_0 \left\{ \sum_{t=0}^{\infty} \beta^t U(c_t, l_t) \right\}, \quad 0 < \beta < 1. \tag{4.51}$$

Households are assumed to own the capital stock and to make investment decisions i_t subject to the resource constraint $c_t + i_t \leq y_t + (1 - \delta)k_t$, where $0 < \delta < 1$ is the depreciation rate on capital. By contrast, firms rent labor, capital, and transactions services to maximize profits on a period-by-period basis. Households are also assumed to combine time and transactions services to accomplish consumption and investment purchases. The time required for this activity is

$$n_{\tau t} = \tau(d_{ht}/(c_t + i_t))(c_t + i_t), \tag{4.52}$$

where $\tau' < 0$, $\tau'' < 0$. The household chooses an amount of transactions services d_{ht} so as to minimize the total transactions costs, $w_t n_{\tau t} + \rho_t d_{ht}$, where w_t is the real wage and ρ_t is the rental price of transactions services. This implies a demand for transactions services that can be obtained from the first-order condition

$$\rho_t = w_t \tau'(d_{ht}/(c_t + i_t)) \tag{4.53}$$

as $d_{ht}^* = h(\rho_t/w_t)(c_t + i_t)$, where $h = (\tau')^{-1}$. Likewise, hours allocated to producing transactions services is $n_{\tau t}^* = \tau^*(h(\rho_t/w_t))(c_t + i_t)$. Finally, we require that the household's time allocated to the different activities sums to 1, $n_t = n_{ft} + n_{dt} + n_{\tau t}$.

This framework can be used to rationalize the observations regarding money and output. Specifically, *inside money*, or a broad measure of money that includes commercial credit, is more closely related to output than *outside money*. Suppose that a shock to the production of final goods or, equivalently, a positive shock to productivity occurs. Then, consumption and leisure of the representative consumer will rise but so will investment demand as consumers seek to spread the extra wealth over time. If the substitution effect of an increase in the marginal product of labor outweighs the wealth effect of the productivity shock, there will be an increase in hours of work. As a consequence, investment demand rises and output will also increase in response to the additional hours worked, so firms will wish to finance a greater volume of goods in process. As a result, commercial credit, or inside money, responds to the positive productivity shock. The increase in output will also stimulate the demand for transactions services by households and firms. Hence, the causality runs from the productivity shock to money even though the increase in money occurs before the higher productivity shock.

Ahmed and Murthy [3] provide a test of this hypothesis using a small open economy such as Canada to evaluate the impact of exogenously given terms of trade and real interest rates versus domestic aggregate demand and supply disturbances. Their results are derived from a structural vector autoregression (VAR) with long-run restrictions to identify the alternative structural shocks. Consistent with the RBC view, they find that an important source of the money-output correlation is output shocks affecting inside money in the short run. Another possibility is that the central bank uses the *accommodative monetary policy*.[9] During an expansion, if interest rates are rising and firms wish to invest more in anticipation of higher expected profits, the central bank may expand the money supply to keep interest rates from rising too rapidly.

3.5. THE SOURCE OF THE SHOCKS

The RBC model has come under much criticism for assuming that technology or productivity shocks are the sole driving force of cyclical fluctuations. One

---

[9] See Sims [190].

way of dealing with this criticism is to introduce alternative sources of shocks into RBC models. In the previous section, we discussed the role of government or fiscal shocks in generating observed co-movements of the data. In this vein, Christiano and Eichenbaum [65] introduce government consumption shocks as a way of breaking the strong and positive relationship between hours worked and productivity implied by the basic RBC model. Other papers that have employed the RBC framework with fiscal shocks include Braun [46] and McGrattan [158]. These authors consider the impact of distortionary taxes on real outcomes. War shocks can also be modeled as a source of cyclical fluctuations (see Barro [27] and Ohanian [169]).[10]

3.5.1. *Investment-Specific Technological Shocks*

An important source of shocks is the investment-specific technological change. This has been examined by Greenwood, Hercowitz, and Krusell [106, 107]. Following Gordon [104], these authors motivate their analysis by noting that, during the period 1950–1990, the relative price of new equipment declined by 3% at an average annual rate while the equipment-GNP ratio increased substantially. Furthermore, there was a negative correlation (-0.46) between a de-trended measure of the relative price of capital and investment expenditures. The notion behind this type of change is that production of capital goods becomes increasingly efficient over time, thereby stimulating output growth.[11]

In Greenwood *et al.* [107], the role of investment-specific technological shocks is used to account for cyclical fluctuations. Consider a standard RBC model with a representative consumer who derives utility from consumption and leisure as

$$E_0 \left\{ \sum_{t=0}^{\infty} \beta^t [\theta \ln (c_t) + (1 - \theta) \ln (1 - l_t)] \right\}, \quad 0 < \theta < 1,$$

---

[10] Altug, Demers, and Demers [10] examine the impact of political risk and regime changes due to changes in the party in power on real investment decisions under irreversibility. Although their analysis is not general equilibrium, they nevertheless show that political events can have non-negligible effects on real economic variables.

[11] In Greenwood, Hercowitz, and Krusell [106], the authors use a growth accounting approach to show that investment-specific shocks can account for 60% of postwar US growth of output per man-hour.

where c_t denotes consumption and l_t denotes labor supply. There is a production technology that depends on labor and the services from two types of capital goods, equipment denoted k_e and structures denoted k_s. Equipment is utilized at the time-varying rate h; hence, the service flow is denoted hk_e. The production function is given by

$$y = F(hk_e, k_s, l, z) = z(hk_e)^{\alpha_e} k_s^{\alpha_s} l^{1-\alpha_e-\alpha_s}, \quad 0 < \alpha_e, \alpha_s, \alpha_e + \alpha_s < 1,$$

where z is a measure of total factor productivity. Structures evolve according to the standard law of motion:

$$k_s' = (1 - \delta_s)k_s + i_i, \quad 0 < \delta_s < 1. \tag{5.54}$$

The law of motion for equipment is given by

$$k_e' = (1 - \delta_e(h))k_e + i_e q, \tag{5.55}$$

where the variable q shows the investment-specific technological change in equipment and

$$\delta_e(h) = \frac{b}{\omega}h, \quad \omega > 1. \tag{5.56}$$

Thus, investment in equipment is subject to variable rates of utilization and depreciation which are convex in the utilization rate. The shocks to technology and to the efficiency of equipment capital constitute the drivers of the model. They evolve as $z_{t+1} = \gamma_z^{t+1} \exp(\zeta_{t+1})$ and $q_{t+1} = \gamma_q^{t+1} \exp(\eta_{t+1})$, where ζ_{t+1} and η_{t+1} are innovations to productivity and investment-specific technological change, respectively, that follow first-order Markov processes, and γ_z and γ_q denote the average gross growth rates of the two processes.

Investment in both structures and equipment is also subject to convex costs of adjustment denoted as $a = a_e + a_s$, where

$$a_e = \exp(\eta)\phi_e(k_e'/q - \kappa_e k_e/q)^2/(k_e q), \quad \phi_e, \kappa_e > 0, \tag{5.57}$$

$$a_s = \phi_s(k_s' - \kappa_s k_s)^2, \quad \phi_s, \kappa_s > 0. \tag{5.58}$$

Finally, there is a government which levies taxes on labor and capital income at the rates τ_l and τ_k, respectively. The revenue raised by the government is returned to the private sector through lump-sum transfers τ. This yields the government budget constraint:

$$\tau = \tau_k(r_e h k_e + r_s k_s) + \tau_l w l, \tag{5.59}$$

where r_e and r_s denote the rental rate on equipment and structures, respectively, and w denotes the real wage rate. The resource constraint requires that consumption plus investment in the two types of capital equal output net of adjustment costs:

$$c + i_e + i_s = y - a_e - a_s. \tag{5.60}$$

In this analysis, the investment-specific technological shock plays a key role. A higher value of q directly affects the quantity of equipment that will be available to produce output next period. However, it also affects the utilization cost of existing equipment this period by lowering the replacement cost of old capital goods, and hence increases its utilization. Hence, investment-specific technological change increases the services from old equipment at the same time as it increases the quantity of equipment available for next period.

We note that the economy displays balanced growth as z_t and q_t grow at the rates γ_z and γ_q, respectively. In the balanced growth path equilibrium, the quantity of labor l and the utilization rate h are constant. The resource constraint and the accumulation equation for structures imply that y, c, i_e, i_s, a_e, a_s, and k_s all have to grow at the same rate; denote this rate by g. Equipment, however, grows faster, at the rate $g_e = \gamma_q g$.[12] A key parameter to be estimated from the data is γ_q. Since the inverse of q denotes the relative price of equipment in terms of consumption goods, this quantity is determined as the ratio of Gordon's [104] price index of quality-adjusted equipment and the price index for consumption. The parameters that are determined using *a priori* information include the average growth rate of the investment-specific shock γ_q, the depreciation rate on structures δ_s, and the tax rate on wage income τ_l. The first parameter is determined using data on the inverse of the relative price of investment goods following Gordon [104], and it is set at

---

[12] From the production function, we have that $g = \gamma_z(\gamma_q g)^{\alpha_e} g^{\alpha_s}$, or

$$g = \gamma_z^{1/(1-\alpha_e-\alpha_s)} \gamma_q^{\alpha_e/(1-\alpha_e-\alpha_s)},$$

$$g_e = \gamma_z^{1/(1-\alpha_e-\alpha_s)} \gamma_q^{(1-\alpha_s)/(1-\alpha_e-\alpha_s)}.$$

1.032. Likewise, $\delta_s = 0.056$ and $\tau_l = 0.40$. The second set of parameters is calculated using information on the long-run behavior of a set of the model's variables. This standard calibration exercise yields $\theta = 0.40$, $\alpha_e = 0.18$, $\alpha_s = 0.12$, $\omega = 1.59$, $\tau_k = 0.53$, $\beta = 0.97$, $g = 1.0124$, and $bh^\omega = 0.20$, where the parameters b and h cannot be identified separately. The restriction that adjustment costs are zero along the balanced growth path yields the values $\kappa_e = \kappa_s = g$. Furthermore, the symmetry condition $\phi_e = (g/g_e)^2 \phi_s \equiv \phi$ leaves only the parameter ϕ to be determined.

The model is simulated to understand the contribution of the investment-specific technological shocks in generating cyclical fluctuations. Hence, only the q shock is assumed to be operative. Unlike the standard technology shock in RBC models, the investment-specific shock affects uses of factors such as labor and capital through changed investment opportunities. A positive shock to this variable works by increasing the rate of return to equipment investment, which tends to raise the stock of equipment next period. Simultaneously, there is a decline in the equipment's replacement value, which raises utilization of equipment today. This leads to increased employment and output. Given that equipment investment is only 7% of GNP and 18% of the value of output being derived from the use of equipment, the fraction of output directly affected by the shock will typically be small. Hence, the impact of the investment-specific technological shock depends on the quantitative importance of the transmission mechanism. For this purpose, Greenwood *et al.* [107] calibrate the adjustment cost parameter under two alternative assumptions. According to the first, the parameter ϕ is set to equalize the consumption/output correlation implied by the model to that in the data. This provides a lower bound on the contribution of the q shocks because a positive shock to q reduces consumption at the same time as it increases investment. A high value of ϕ works to reduce investment and to increase the procyclicality of consumption. By contrast, a low value of the adjustment cost parameter ϕ is chosen to make the volatility of investment in the model equal to that in the data. This constitutes an upper value for the contribution of the shocks q. They find that under a high value of ϕ, the investment-specific technological shocks explain around 28% of business cycle fluctuations as captured by the standard deviation of output. For a low value of ϕ, this figure is 32%. They conclude that though investment-specific shocks contribute to business cycle fluctuations, they are not the main factor.

3.5.2. *Energy Shocks*

From the beginning, the source of large supply-side shocks for the RBC agenda has been sought in oil shocks. Barsky and Kilian [28] analyze the relationship between oil shocks and changes in economic activity. Rotemberg and Woodford [183] provide a rationale for the role of energy price shocks in a model with imperfect competition. By contrast, Finn [92] argues that it is possible to rationalize the role of energy shocks in models with perfect competition. In her model, capital utilization is the channel through which energy shocks enter the model. We briefly describe her model before concluding this chapter.

As in the standard RBC framework, there is a representative consumer with preferences:

$$E_0 \left\{ \sum_{t=0}^{\infty} \beta^t u(c_t, l_t) \right\}, \quad 0 < \beta < 1,$$

with

$$u(c_t, l_t) = \frac{\left[c_t^{\alpha} (1 - l_t)^{1-\alpha} \right]^{1-\sigma} - 1}{1 - \sigma}, \quad 0 < \alpha < 1, \quad \sigma > 0.$$

The production function is given by

$$y_t = (z_t l_t)^{\theta} (k_t u_t)^{1-\theta}, \quad 0 < \theta < 1,$$

where z_t is an exogenous technology shock, k_t is the stock of capital, and u_t is the rate of utilization of capital. As in the previous model, the depreciation of physical capital depends on its utilization rate so that

$$k_{t+1} = (1 - \delta(u_t))k_t + i_t, \quad \delta(u_t) = \frac{\omega_0 u_t^{\omega_1}}{\omega_1},$$

where $0 < \delta(u_t) < 1$, $\omega_0 > 0$, and $\omega_1 > 1$. The new feature in Finn's analysis is that capital utilization requires energy:

$$\frac{e_t}{k_t} = \frac{v_0 u_t^{v_1}}{v_1}, \quad v_0 > 0, \quad v_1 > 1.$$

We can solve this equation for the utilization rate u_t and substitute it into the production function to obtain

$$y_t = (z_t l_t)^\theta \left[k_t^{1 - \frac{1}{v_1}} e_t^{\frac{1}{v_1}} \left(\frac{v_1}{v_0} \right)^{\frac{1}{v_1}} \right]^{1-\theta}.$$

Thus, the production of output depends on labor, capital, and energy. This shows the *direct* effect of energy, but there is also an *indirect* effect which works through the effect of the utilization rate on the depreciation of capital. Hence, there are two channels for the transmission of energy shocks in the model. Finally, the economy-wide resource constraint is given by

$$c_t + i_t + p_t e_t \le y_t,$$

where p_t is the price of energy.

Finn [92] describes qualitatively and quantitatively the impact of increases in the price of energy. First, an increase in p_t reduces e_t and u_t through the production function. The decrease in e_t further reduces the marginal product of labor, and hence the real wage w_t and work effort l_t. Thus, a positive energy price shock operates in a similar way as a negative technology shock. If the price shock is persistent, then the decrease in the values of e_t, u_t, and l_t continue into the future and reduce the future marginal productivity of capital. This tends to reduce the investment i_t and the future capital stock k_t. The indirect effect of the increase in the price of energy on capital's future marginal energy cost also tends to reduce investment and the future capital stock. Finn [92] shows that the quantitative response of value-added and real wages to a shock in energy prices implied by the model is in line with that in the data.

Chapter 4
International Business Cycles

The international business cycle literature provides an extension to the original real business cycle (RBC) approach by allowing for open-economy considerations. One of the aims of the RBC approach has been to determine whether two-country versions of the basic model can account for both the co-movements studied in closed-economy models as well as international co-movements, including correlations of macroeconomic aggregates across countries and movements in the balance of trade. The closed-economy model cannot be used to understand the propagation of shocks across countries or regions, nor can it be used to discuss notions of international risk sharing. Unlike the closed-economy model, open-economy business cycle models allow for the role of technology processes in different countries in generating cyclical fluctuations. They can be used to model the impact of the ability to trade in goods and to borrow and lend internationally. In this chapter, we review some of the facts of international business cycles and discuss models that have been used to rationalize the findings.

4.1. FACTS

One of the important areas of research has been to derive the so-called stylized facts of international business cycles. Backus, Kehoe, and Kydland [25] consider data on 12 developed countries over a sample period dating from 1960 to 1990. They consider a two-country RBC model that has the features of the original Kydland–Prescott model and that assumes a single homogeneous good and complete contingent claims for allocating risk. They study the properties of a baseline model against the actual features in the data. Backus *et al.* [26] study the properties of the same model for ten developed countries plus a European aggregate developed by the OECD between 1970 and 1990. The individual countries they consider are Australia, Austria, Canada, France, Germany, Italy, Japan, Switzerland, the United Kingdom, and the United States. The data are filtered using the Hodrick–Prescott filter. Among the important features of their analysis is the estimation of the correlation properties of international productivity shocks using data on estimated Solow residuals. Thus, the exercise in this literature is to replicate the correlation properties among the different series *given* the variability and correlation properties of the shocks. In this regard, Backus *et al.* [25, 26] estimate a bivariate AR(1) process for the domestic and foreign shocks as

$$\begin{bmatrix} z_t \\ z_t^* \end{bmatrix} = A \begin{bmatrix} z_{t-1} \\ z_{t-1}^* \end{bmatrix} + \begin{bmatrix} \epsilon_t \\ \epsilon_t^* \end{bmatrix},$$

where z_t, z_t^* denote the technology shocks to the domestic and foreign countries, respectively, and ϵ_t, ϵ_t^* denote the respective innovations to these shocks. Based on several estimated specifications for the US and the European aggregate, these authors use a symmetric specification with

$$A = \begin{bmatrix} 0.906 & 0.088 \\ 0.088 & 0.906 \end{bmatrix},$$

with $Std(\epsilon_t) = Std(\epsilon_t^*) = 0.00852$ and $Corr(\epsilon_t, \epsilon_t^*) = 0.258$. The positive off-diagonal entries allow for spillover effects of the shock to productivity in one country to have a positive effect on the productivity of the other country. The large autoregressive coefficients displayed on the diagonal capture the persistence in observed productivity.

The findings can be summarized under two headings:

- *The quantity anomaly*: In the data, the cross-country correlations of output are greater than those of productivity, measured as the Solow residual, and the cross-correlations of productivity are greater than those of consumption. By contrast, the theoretical model implies the reverse ranking.
- *The price anomaly*: The volatility of the terms of trade, defined as the relative price of imports to exports, is much higher in the data than it is in the theoretical model.

Ambler, Cardia, and Zimmermann [14] extend the Backus *et al.* [26] sample to 20 industrialized countries over the period 1960–2004. They estimate the moments of interest using the generalized method of moments (GMM) estimation, which allows them to obtain standard errors. The findings of Ambler *et al.* [14] confirm the findings of Backus *et al.* [25, 26], though with lower magnitudes. They also find that the cross-country correlations of output, investment, and employment are positive and generally high in the data; whereas in the model, they are negative.

The international RBC model produces these results because it implies that the incentive is to use inputs where they are most productive. This fact leads to negative cross-correlations between output, investment, and employment in the theoretical model. In other words, suppose a positive technology shock occurs in one country, say, the US. This leads to a strong investment response in the US, which is accompanied by output and employment increases. Since investment responds strongly to a positive productivity shock, the increase in investment plus consumption is greater than the increase in output, which leads to a trade deficit in the domestic country. In a model with perfect capital mobility, we thus observe a flow of factors from other countries or regions to the US. By contrast, what is typically observed in the data are *positive* co-movements in these series across countries. Furthermore, investment and the trade balance are more volatile in the model than they are in the data. The two-country frictionless international business cycle model also implies that consumers in different countries can share risk perfectly. This feature of the model leads to the cross-country correlations of consumption being much higher in the model than in the data. The price anomaly arises because the real exchange rate in the baseline international RBC model is closely related to the ratio of consumption across the two countries. With perfect risk sharing, this ratio displays little volatility, implying that the real exchange rate is also less volatile in the model than it is in the data.

In their original analysis, Backus *et al.* [25] also examine a variety of perturbations of their original setup. First, they consider *asymmetric spillovers* between the US and the European aggregate in which the response of US productivity to shocks to European productivity is *smaller* than the response of European productivity to shocks to US productivity. This changes the output-investment correlation from positive to negative in the domestic country, but the variability of investment and the trade balance continue to remain counterfactually high, as does the positive correlation of consumption across countries. Second, they consider large spillovers across countries by changing the off-diagonal elements of the *A* matrix from 0.088 to 0.2 and the correlation of the innovations from 0.258 to 0.5. With this change, they find that investment and the trade balance become much less volatile, and the cross-country correlation of output goes from being negative to positive. However, the cross-country correlation of consumption increases further. They also examine various sorts of *trading frictions*. The first of these involves introducing a small trading friction in the form of a *transport cost*. They find that this friction has the effect of reducing the volatility of investment and the trade balance, but has little effect on the cross-country correlations of consumption and output. Next, they eliminate all trade in goods and assets by considering an *autarky* situation. In this case, it is the correlation between technology shocks that leads to any connection between countries. They find that the results are very similar to the case with a small transport cost. Surprisingly, elimination of trade in state-contingent claims does not help to lower the cross-country correlations of consumption. Backus *et al.* [25] argue that this result is not due to international risk sharing considerations, but stems from the permanent income hypothesis: when domestic and foreign productivity shocks are correlated, a rise in productivity in the domestic country signals a rise in productivity in the foreign country through the spillover effects. Hence, the foreign agent increases consumption and reduces investment in anticipation of future income increases.

4.2. THE ROLE OF INTERNATIONAL RISK SHARING

Before we continue with other extensions that have been proposed in the international RBC literature, it is important to understand the role of alternative financial arrangements in generating the cross-country correlations. Cole [71] argued that it is important to examine how alternative financial arrangements interact with the preferences and the production possibilities set to determine the behavior of the real variables. The standard international RBC model studied by Backus *et al.* [25, 26] considers the case with complete contingent claims and perfect risk sharing across different countries. Cole [71] and Cole and Obstfeld [72] examine a two-country real version of the Lucas asset pricing model for this purpose (see Lucas [152]). Agents from both countries are identical in terms of preferences and differ only in terms of endowments. There are two goods, Y_1 and Y_2. Country 1 has a random endowment of good Y_1 and country 2 has a random endowment of good Y_2. Neither good is storable. We assume that endowments are stationary in levels.

Let $s_t \in S \subseteq \mathbf{R}_+^m$ denote a vector of exogenous shocks that follows a discrete first-order Markov process with a stationary probability transition matrix P with (i,j) element $p_{i,j}$, where $p_{i,j} = p(s_t = s_j|s_{t-1} = s_i)$. Let $\hat{\pi}$ denote the vector of stationary probabilities which satisfy $\hat{\pi} = P'\hat{\pi}$. In the beginning, agents observe the current realization. We assume that endowment is a time-invariant function of the exogenous shock.

Assumption 2.1. *Define* $\mathcal{Y} \equiv [\underline{y}, \bar{y}]$, *where* $\underline{y} > 0$ *and* $\bar{y} < \infty$. *The functions* $y_1 : S \to \mathcal{Y}$ *and* $y_2 : S \to \mathcal{Y}$ *are continuous functions that are bounded away from zero.*

The representative consumer in country j has preferences over random sequences $\{c_{1,t}^j, c_{2,t}^j\}_{t=0}^{\infty}$ defined by

$$E_0 \left\{ \sum_{t=0}^{\infty} \beta^t U(c_{1,t}^j, c_{2,t}^j) \right\}, \quad 0 < \beta < 1. \tag{2.1}$$

We have the following assumption.

Assumption 2.2. *The utility function* $U : \mathbf{R}_+^2 \to \mathbf{R}$ *is continuously differentiable, strictly increasing, and strictly concave. For all* $c_1, c_2 > 0$,

$$\lim_{c_1 \to 0} \frac{U_1(c_1, c_2)}{U_2(c_1, c_2)} = \infty, \quad \lim_{c_2 \to 0} \frac{U_1(c_1, c_2)}{U_2(c_1, c_2)} = 0.$$

This requirement on the utility function ensures that both goods are consumed in equilibrium.

4.2.1. *Pareto Optimal Allocations*

We begin by characterizing the Pareto optimal allocations. To do this, we can examine the solution to a central planning problem which maximizes the weighted utility of agents in the domestic and foreign countries subject to the resource constraints. Let ϕ_j denote the Pareto weight for country j. Define

$$\pi(s^t) = \pi(s_t|s_{t-1})\pi(s_{t-1}|s_{t-2})\cdots\pi(s_1|s_0)\hat{\pi}(s_0),$$

where $s^t = (s_t, s_{t-1}, \ldots, s_0)$ denotes the history of the shocks at time t. The social planner chooses sequences $\{c_i^1(s^t), c_i^2(s^t)\}_{t=0}^{\infty}$ to maximize the weighted sum of utilities subject to the sequence of resource constraints

$$\sum_{t=0}^{\infty}\sum_{s^t}\pi(s^t)\beta^t\left[\phi_1 U(c_1^1(s^t), c_2^1(s^t)) + \phi_2 U(c_1^2(s^t), c_2^2(s^t))\right] \qquad (2.2)$$

subject to

$$c_i^1(s^t) + c_i^2(s^t) = y_i(s_t), \quad i = 1, 2.$$

Since preferences are time-separable, the endowment is nonstorable, and there is no investment process, the social planner's problem at time t involves solving the static problem

$$\max[\phi_1 U(c_{1,t}^1, c_{2,t}^1) + \phi_2 U(c_{1,t}^2, c_{2,t}^2)] \qquad (2.3)$$

subject to

$$c_{i,t}^1 + c_{i,t}^2 = y_{i,t}, \quad i = 1, 2,$$

where $c_{i,t}^j$ denotes the consumption of good i by residents of country j. Let $\mu_i(s_t)$ denote the Lagrange multiplier for the resource constraint for good i. The first-order conditions imply that

$$\phi_j U_1(c_{1,t}^j, c_{2,t}^j) = \mu_1(s_t),$$

$$\phi_j U_2(c_{1,t}^j, c_{2,t}^j) = \mu_2(s_t)$$

for $j = 1, 2$, or

$$\frac{U_1(c_{1,t}^1, c_{2,t}^1)}{U_1(c_{1,t}^2, c_{2,t}^2)} = \frac{\phi_2}{\phi_1}, \qquad (2.4)$$

$$\frac{U_2(c_{1,t}^1, c_{2,t}^1)}{U_2(c_{1,t}^2, c_{2,t}^2)} = \frac{\phi_2}{\phi_1}. \qquad (2.5)$$

Hence, we find that the ratio of marginal utilities across agents in different countries is equalized for all states and goods. This is an implication of *perfect risk sharing* that arises in a complete contingent claims equilibrium.

It is convenient to assume that preferences are of the Cobb–Douglas variety:

$$U(c_{1,t}, c_{2,t}) = \frac{(c_{1,t}^{\alpha} c_{2,t}^{1-\alpha})^{1-\rho}}{1-\rho}. \tag{2.6}$$

Assuming that preferences are of Cobb–Douglas variety, the Pareto optimal consumption allocations satisfy

$$c_{1,t}^1 = \delta y_{1,t} \tag{2.7}$$

$$c_{2,t}^1 = \delta y_{2,t} \tag{2.8}$$

$$c_{1,t}^2 = (1-\delta)y_{1,t} \tag{2.9}$$

$$c_{2,t}^2 = (1-\delta)y_{2,t}, \tag{2.10}$$

where

$$\delta = \left[1 + \left(\frac{\phi_2}{\phi_1}\right)^{\sigma}\right]$$

and $o = \frac{1}{\rho}$.

These expressions show that consumers in each country consume a constant fraction of output in each period. Also note that a shock to the output of country 1, which also causes the output of country 2 to increase through positive spillover effects, will cause consumption in both countries to increase. This implication of the model has been shown to lead to the counterfactually high cross-country correlations of consumption implied by the standard international RBC model. In what follows, we will examine the role of alternative financial arrangements that can be used to rationalize the observations.

4.2.2. *Complete Contingent Claims*

Consider first the behavior of allocations in a competitive equilibrium in which agents can trade claims that pay off contingent on all possible realizations of the income processes in each country. It is straightforward to demonstrate that there exists a contingent claims equilibrium for this economy, and that the competitive equilibrium allocations are Pareto optimal.

Consider first the case when agents can trade one-period contingent claims that pay off in each state next period on the consumption good of each country. Given the Markov nature of uncertainty, it is without loss of generality to consider only one-period contingent claims.[1] Agents can also trade in the goods of the other country. Let $p(s_t)$ denote the relative price of good y_2 in terms of the numéraire good y_1. The sequential budget constraints for residents of country j for $j = 1, 2$ are given by

$$y_{1,t} + z_{1,t}^1 + p(s_t)z_{2,t}^1 = c_{1,t}^1 + p(s_t)c_{2,t}^1$$

$$+ \sum_{s_{t+1} \in S} q(s_{t+1}, s_t) \left[z_1^1(s_{t+1}) + p(s_t)z_2^1(s_{t+1}) \right] \qquad (2.11)$$

$$y_{2,t} + \frac{z_{1,t}^2}{p(s_t)} + z_{2,t}^2 = \frac{c_{1,t}^2}{p(s_t)} + c_{2,t}^2$$

$$+ \sum_{s_{t+1} \in S} q(s_{t+1}, s_t) \left[\frac{z_1^2(s_{t+1})}{p(s_t)} + z_2^2(s_{t+1}) \right], \qquad (2.12)$$

where $q(s_{t+1}, s_t)$ is the price of a contingent claim that pays off in each possible state next period conditional on the state today and $z_i^j(s_{t+1})$ are the holdings of country i's assets by consumers from country j for $i, j = 1, 2$. Thus, these equations indicate that the output produced in country 1 plus the receipts (or payments) on assets denominated in the goods of countries 1 and 2 must be equal to consumption of domestic goods plus imports of foreign goods plus purchases (sales) of contingent assets denominated in the goods of countries 1 and 2.

The current account for each country, denoted as CA^j, is given by

$$CA^1 = y_{1,t} - \left(c_{1,t}^1 + p(s_t)c_{2,t}^1 \right),$$

$$CA^2 = y_{2,t} - \left(\frac{c_{1,t}^2}{p(s_t)} + c_{2,t}^2 \right),$$

---

[1] For further discussion, see Altug and Labadie [6], Ch. 7.

and the capital account denoted KA^j is given by

$$KA^1 = z_{1,t}^1 + p(s_t)z_{2,t}^1 - \sum_{s_{t+1} \in S} q(s_{t+1}, s_t) \left(z_1^1(s_{t+1}) + p(s_t)z_2^1(s_{t+1}) \right),$$

$$KA^2 = \frac{z_{1,t}^2}{p(s_t)} + z_{2,t}^2 - \sum_{s_{t+1} \in S} q(s_{t+1}, s_t) \left(\frac{z_1^2(s_{t+1})}{p(s_t)} + z_2^2(s_{t+1}) \right).$$

We can interpret the budget constraints for each country j by stating that the sum of the current account plus the capital account must be zero:

$$CA^j + KA^j = 0, \quad j = 1, 2.$$

In an economy with trade in international assets, a current account deficit ($CA < 0$) must be balanced with a capital account surplus ($KA > 0$). This implies that a country which consumes more than it produces must be a net borrower or, equivalently, it must sell more assets to the rest of the world than it purchases from the rest of the world.

The market-clearing conditions are given by

$$c_{i,t}^1 + c_{i,t}^2 = y_{i,t},$$

$$z_{i,t}^1 + z_{i,t}^2 - 0,$$

$$z_i^1(s_{t+1}) + z_i^2(s_{t+1}) = 0, \quad s_{t+1} \in S$$

for $i = 1, 2$.

Given the Markov nature of uncertainty, we can define the value function for the problem of each consumer in country j as

$$V\left(s_t, z_{1,t}^j, z_{2,t}^j\right) = \max_{\{c_{i,t}^j, z_{i,t+1}^j\}_{i=1,2}} \left\{ U\left(c_{1,t}^j, c_{2,t}^j\right) \right.$$

$$\left. + \beta \sum_{s_{t+1} \in S} \pi(s_{t+1}|s_t) V\left(s_{t+1}, z_{1,t+1}^j, z_{2,t+1}^j\right) \right\}$$

subject to the budget constraint (2.11) (or (2.12)). Let $\lambda^i(s_t)$ denote the Lagrange multiplier for country i in state s_t. The first-order conditions with envelope conditions substituted in are given by

$$U_1(c_{1,t}^1, c_{2,t}^1) = \lambda^1(s_t),$$

$$U_2(c_{1,t}^1, c_{2,t}^1) = p(s_t)\lambda^1(s_t),$$

$$U_1(c_{1,t}^2, c_{2,t}^2) = \frac{\lambda^2(s_t)}{p(s_t)},$$

$$U_2(c_{1,t}^2, c_{2,t}^2) = \lambda^2(s_t),$$

$$\lambda^i(s_t)q(s_{t+1}, s_t) = \beta\pi(s_{t+1}|s_t)\lambda^i(s_{t+1}), \quad i = 1, 2.$$

Simplifying these conditions yields

$$\frac{U_2(c_{1,t}^i, c_{2,t}^i)}{U_1(c_{1,t}^i, c_{2,t}^i)} = p(s_t), \quad i = 1, 2 \qquad (2.13)$$

and

$$\frac{\beta\pi(s_{t+1}|s_t)U_1(c_{1,t+1}^i, c_{2,t+1}^i)}{U_1(c_{1,t}^i, c_{2,t}^i)} = q(s_{t+1}, s_t), \quad i = 1, 2. \qquad (2.14)$$

Thus, we see that the Pareto optimal allocations can be supported in a complete contingent claims equilibrium if

$$\lambda^i(s_t) = \frac{\mu^i(s_t)}{\phi^i}, \quad i = 1, 2, \quad \text{where } p(s_t) = \frac{\mu^2(s_t)}{\mu^1(s_t)}.$$

In this equilibrium, we find that consumers in each country equate their marginal rates of substitution for each good across all possible current states.

If preferences satisfy the Cobb–Douglas assumption, then consumers in each country consume a constant fraction of current output as specified in equations (2.7)–(2.10). This follows from the fact that the competitive equilibrium is Pareto optimal. Hence,

$$p(s_t) = \frac{(1-\alpha)c_{1,t}^i}{\alpha c_{2,t}^i} = \frac{(1-\alpha)y_{1,t}}{\alpha y_{2,t}}.$$

In this case, the contingent claims contracts are considered to be consistent with the results on consumption for each country. Given the solution for the relative price $p(s_t)$ and the consumption allocations given in equations (2.7)–(2.10), notice that the solution

$$z_1^i(s_{t+1}) = z_2^i(s_{t+1}) = 0, \quad z_{1,t}^i = z_{2,t}^i = 0$$

with $\delta = \alpha$ satisfies the consumers' budget constraints and the market-clearing conditions. But this is a contingent claims equilibrium in which no assets are traded! In such an equilibrium, it is still possible to price the contingent claims using the expression in (2.14). In the next section, we will demonstrate explicitly that the Pareto optimal allocations can indeed be attained in a no-asset-trading equilibrium. Since the price of any financial asset can be obtained as a function of the contingent claims prices, it follows that any financial asset can also be priced in such an equilibrium.

4.2.3. *No Asset Trading*

Now suppose that there is trade in goods but no trade in international assets. In this case, we are forcing the current account to equal zero in each period. Country 1 and 2's budget constraints can be expressed, respectively, as

$$c_{1,t}^1 + p_t c_{2,t}^1 = y_{1,t}, \tag{2.15}$$

$$\frac{c_{1,t}^2}{p_t} + c_{2,t}^2 = y_{2,t}. \tag{2.16}$$

Once again, this is a static problem because there are no assets for intertemporal consumption smoothing and the endowment is nonstorable. Let μ_t^j denote the Lagrange multiplier on the budget constraint of country j. If we assume the Cobb–Douglas functional form for preferences, then the consumption allocations are

$$c_{1,t}^1 = \alpha y_{1,t},$$

$$c_{2,t}^1 = \frac{(1 - \alpha)y_{1,t}}{p_t},$$

$$c_{1,t}^2 = \alpha p_t y_{2,t},$$

$$c_{2,t}^2 = (1 - \alpha)y_{2,t}.$$

Equilibrium in the two goods markets requires that

$$c_{1,t}^1 + c_{1,t}^2 = y_{1,t}, \tag{2.17}$$

$$c_{2,t}^1 + c_{2,t}^2 = y_{2,t}. \tag{2.18}$$

Substitute the consumption functions into the market-clearing conditions and solve for the relative price to show that

$$p_t = \frac{(1-\alpha)y_{1,t}}{\alpha y_{2,t}}.$$

This price can be substituted into the consumption functions above to show that

$$c_{2,t}^1 = \alpha y_{2,t},$$

$$c_{1,t}^2 = (1-\alpha)y_{1,t}.$$

Notice that the no-asset-trading allocation is identical to the central planning allocation if

$$\alpha = \delta = \left[1 + \left(\frac{\phi_2}{\phi_1}\right)^\sigma\right],$$

or

$$\phi^1 = \left[1 + \left(\frac{1-\alpha}{\alpha}\right)^\rho\right]^{-1}$$

and $\phi^2 = 1 - \phi^1$.

This exercise illustrates several points:

- The absence of international capital mobility does not necessarily imply that the allocation is not Pareto optimal. Efficient risk sharing can occur despite the lack of financial assets and insurance.
- The international ratio of marginal utilities across countries is identical across goods and states. A large and positive shock in the amount of good $y_{1,t}$ is positively transmitted to the residents of country 2 by the increase in demand (and hence the relative price) for good $y_{2,t}$. A large negative shock in the amount of a good is similarly transmitted across borders, despite the absence of trade in financial assets. Hence, efficient risk sharing occurs through changes in the relative price of goods.

- Notice that we can price financial assets in the model, under the assumption that the current account is zero, and can show that real interest rates and real asset returns will be equal for the two countries, despite the absence of financial capital mobility.
- The total consumption of countries 1 and 2 is

$$c_{1,t}^1 + p_t c_{2,t}^1 = \alpha y_{1,t} + \alpha y_{2,t},$$

$$c_{1,t}^2 + p_t c_{2,t}^2 = (1 - \alpha) y_{1,t} + (1 - \alpha) y_{2,t}.$$

Notice that correlation of the total value of consumption of country 1 and country 2 is positive and equal to one.

As Cole and Obstfeld [72] point out, the positive transmission of shocks occurs because countries *specialize* in the production of goods.

4.2.4. *Nonspecialization in Endowments*

To illustrate the impact of nonspecialization, Cole and Obstfeld [72] introduce a third good w. Call this third good w. Assume that both countries receive an exogenous and stochastic endowment of good w and let $w^j : S \to W = [\underline{w}, \bar{w}]$ denote the realization of good w in country j. Let $\alpha_1, \alpha_2, \alpha_w$ denote the expenditure shares under the assumption of Cobb–Douglas preferences and let w be the numéraire good, so that $p_{1,t}$ denotes the relative price of good $y_{1,t}$ in terms of w_t and $p_{2,t}$ denotes the relative price of good $y_{2,t}$ in units of w_t. Agents in countries 1 and 2 have budget constraints given, respectively, by

$$p_{1,t} c_{1,t}^1 + p_{2,t} c_{2,t}^1 + c_{w,t}^1 \le p_{1,t} y_{1,t} + w_t^a,$$

$$p_{1,t} c_{1,t}^2 + p_{2,t} c_{2,t}^2 + c_{w,t}^2 \le p_{2,t} y_{2,t} + w_t^b.$$

The equilibrium relative prices satisfy

$$p_{1,t} = \frac{\alpha_1 [w_t^1 + w_t^2]}{\alpha_w y_{1,t}},$$

$$p_{2,t} = \frac{\alpha_2 [w_t^1 + w_t^2]}{\alpha_w y_{2,t}}.$$

The consumption of good 1 by agents in countries 1 and 2, under the assumption of Cobb–Douglas preferences, can be shown to satisfy

$$c_{1,t}^1 = \left[\alpha_w \left(\frac{w_t^1}{w_t^1 + w_t^2} \right) + \alpha_1 \right] y_{1,t},$$

$$c_{1,t}^2 = \left[\alpha_w \left(\frac{w_t^2}{w_t^1 + w_t^2} \right) + \alpha_2 \right] y_{1,t}.$$

Similar expressions can be derived for the consumption of goods y_2 and w. The ratio of marginal utilities of both countries for each good will be equal to a constant across all states, a condition for Pareto optimality, only if the share of the endowment of w_t, $(\frac{w_t^1}{w_t^1 + w_t^2})$ and $(\frac{w_t^2}{w_t^1 + w_t^2})$, is constant as the total w_t varies with s_t. The shocks to w_t^1 and w_t^2 must be perfectly correlated for the allocation with no trade in financial assets to be Pareto optimal. If these shocks are not perfectly correlated, then it is beneficial to trade equity shares or other forms of financial assets.

This helps to clearly distinguish between country-specific shocks, which affect all sectors within a country, and industry-specific shocks. Shocks to $y_{1,t}$ or $y_{2,t}$ are, by definition, country-specific shocks; whereas shocks to w_t^1, w_t^2, where w_t^1, w_t^2 are not perfectly correlated, are sector-specific shocks. Hence, when there are sector-specific shocks, there are gains to asset trading that improve risk sharing and allow diversification. The intuition is that, in the absence of trade in financial assets, the country with a negative shock to the endowment of w_t would like to run a current account deficit by importing w_t and borrowing against future endowment. Since the current account must always be balanced, the country must export more of the good in which it specializes in production to finance the import of good w_t. Notice that the relative price of w_t may not adjust much if w_t^1 and w_t^2 are negatively correlated but the sum $w_t^1 + w_t^2$ fluctuates very little.

4.2.5. *Nontraded Goods*

Suppose now that the third good is a nontraded good. Call this good n and assume that $n^j : S \rightarrow N = [\underline{n}, \bar{n}]$ denotes the realization of good n in country j. Let $\alpha_1, \alpha_2, \alpha_n$ denote the expenditure shares under the assumption of Cobb–Douglas preferences and let y_1 be the numéraire good. Under the assumption of balanced trade and Cobb–Douglas preferences, the demands for the goods satisfy

$$c_{1,t}^1 = \frac{\alpha_1}{1 - \alpha_n} y_{1,t},$$

$$c_{2,t}^1 = \frac{\alpha_1}{1 - \alpha_n} y_{2,t},$$

$$c_{1,t}^2 = \frac{\alpha_2}{1 - \alpha_n} y_{1,t},$$

$$c_{2,t}^2 = \frac{\alpha_2}{1 - \alpha_n} y_{2,t}.$$

Each country consumes its endowment of the nontraded good, n_t^1, n_t^2. The ratio of marginal utility across countries for a traded good will now depend on the ratio $\frac{n_t^1}{n_t^2}$. Unless n_t^1, n_t^2 are perfectly correlated, then the resulting allocations will not be Pareto optimal. There are gains from international risk sharing through asset trade. Notice that the correlation of consumption across countries will now depend on the proportion of a country's consumption that is nontradeable. If this sector constitutes a large fraction of consumption, then even if consumption of traded goods is perfectly correlated, the correlation of national consumption levels may be close to zero. Thus, nontraded goods provide one vehicle for reducing the large cross-country correlations implied by the baseline model.

4.2.6. *Trade in Equity Shares*

We now introduce trade in financial assets. An agent in country 1 holds equity shares that are claims to the endowment stream for good y_1 (the domestic good) and claims to y_2 (the foreign good). We now discuss the impact of asset trading and relate it to the model without asset trade discussed earlier.

Let $z_{i,t}^j$ for $j = 1, 2$ and $i = 1, 2$ denote the shares of good i held by an agent in country j at the beginning of period t. An agent's budget constraint is

$$z_{1,t}^j [y_{1,t} + q_{1,t}] + z_{2,t}^j [p_{2,t} y_{2,t} + q_{2,t}^j]$$
$$\geq c_{1,t}^j + p_{2,t} c_{2,t}^j + q_{1,t} z_{1,t+1}^j + q_{2,t} z_{2,t+1}^j. \qquad (2.19)$$

Let μ_t^j denote the Lagrange multiplier. The agent maximizes his objective function subject to the constraint. The first-order conditions are

$$U_1(c_{1,t}^j, c_{2,t}^j) = U_2(c_{1,t}^j, c_{2,t}^j)p_{2,t}, \tag{2.20}$$

$$U_1(c_{1,t}^j, c_{2,t}^j)q_{1,t} = \beta E_t U_1(c_{1,t+1}^j, c_{2,t+1}^j)[q_{1,t+1} + y_{1,t+1}], \tag{2.21}$$

$$U_1(c_{1,t}^j, c_{2,t}^j)q_{2,t} = \beta E_t U_1(c_{1,t+1}^j, c_{2,t+1}^j)[q_{2,t+1} + p_{2,t+1}y_{2,t+1}]. \tag{2.22}$$

In equilibrium, all equity shares are held and the endowment of each good is completely consumed. Lucas [152] assumes that agents hold identical portfolios, so that $z_{i,t}^j = 1/2$ for $j = 1, 2$ and $i = 1, 2$ so that $\phi^j = 1/2$ and $\delta = 1/2$. In such a world, national wealth is equal across countries and agents have perfectly diversified portfolios. Agents across countries have identical consumption in this case, unlike the economy in which there is no trade in financial assets. In the initial model described earlier, there was no trade in financial assets and specialization in endowments and the allocation was Pareto optimal. We commented that we could price financial assets even if these assets were not traded. If we assume that $z_{1,t}^1 = z_{2,t}^1 = \alpha$ and $z_{1,t}^2 = z_{2,t}^2 = 1 - \alpha$, then the equilibrium allocation with no trade in financial assets can be achieved. Hence, we can achieve at least two stationary allocations, depending on the initial distribution of the claims. This simple example, when combined with our discussion of the equilibrium with no trade in financial assets, illustrates an important point. International risk sharing can be achieved through fluctuations in relative prices in the current account and by trade in financial assets. In particular, it does not require the existence of a full set of contingent claims. The presence of nontraded goods or lack of specialization in production of a good can affect how much consumption insurance can be achieved through relative price fluctuations. If we introduced trade in equity shares when there is a third good w that is produced by both countries, then portfolio diversification may require that an agent hold equity shares for w^1 and w^2 if the endowment shocks for w are not perfectly correlated. If these shocks are perfectly correlated, then portfolio diversification may be achieved by specializing in the holding of equity shares of one country only.

There has been substantial literature on the lack of international portfolio diversification and the degree of international consumption risk sharing. The *international portfolio diversification* puzzle is the notion that investors hold too little of their wealth in foreign securities to be consistent with the standard theory of portfolio choice. Baxter and Jermann [36] argue that the failure of international diversification is substantial. Their model incorporates human and physical capital and, within the context of their model, optimal behavior would lead to a short position in domestic assets because of a strong positive correlation between the returns to human and physical capital. A more recent paper by Heathcote and Perri [117] extends the Baxter and Jermann model to include more than one traded good. They find, as we have noted above, that consumption insurance is available through relative price fluctuations and that these price fluctuations are capable of achieving efficient risk sharing. Clearly, the conclusion on whether there is sufficient or insufficient risk sharing is very sensitive to model specifications.

Empirical evidence on international consumption risk sharing is provided in Backus *et al.* [25], who show that the data are inconsistent with the implications for consumption for the baseline international RBC model. By contrast, Devereux, Gregory, and Smith [81] show that preferences that display a nonseparability between consumption and leisure can help to reduce the consumption correlations implied by the model. Lewis [145] also documents that there is insufficient intertemporal risk sharing in consumption. As we have noted above, the existence of nontraded goods, combined with the assumption that utility is nonseparable in traded and nontraded goods, makes it more difficult to determine the optimal degree of consumption risk sharing. We have also shown above that relative price fluctuations can be a substitute for trade in financial assets in achieving consumption insurance. Lewis [145] documents that the nonseparability of utility or the restriction of asset trade alone is not enough to explain the risk sharing that we observe, but that when nonseparability and asset trade restrictions are combined, she cannot reject the hypothesis that there is risk sharing.

4.2.7. *Limited Risk Sharing*

As described earlier, whether there exists perfect risk sharing in the data appears to depend on the model specification adopted by the researcher. Nevertheless, one could ask whether limited risk sharing opportunities among consumers in different countries could help to better reconcile the data with the model.

In this vein, credit market frictions and restrictions on international capital flows constitute a proposed channel for the propagation of international shocks. Kollman [136] and Baxter and Crucini [34] examine models where only non-contingent bonds can be traded internationally. These authors find that incomplete asset markets help to reduce the cross-country correlation of consumption, but the cross-country correlations of output, investment, and hours worked remain counterfactually negative. Moreover, the results for the cross-country correlations are obtained only if the productivity shocks are highly persistent and there are very little spillover effects across countries. Heathcote and Perri [117] examine the implications of a two-country model under alternative assumptions about the financial structure, given a trade structure. They show that the model matches the correlations in the data under a financial autarky assumption. Their analysis involves extending the analysis in Cole and Obstfeld [72] to incorporate an explicit production side.

Kehoe and Perri [126] consider a model where market incompleteness is obtained endogenously through the introduction of imperfectly enforceable international loans. In their framework, a country can incur international indebtedness only to the extent that such indebtedness can be enforced through the threat of exclusion from future intertemporal and interstate trade. This analysis builds on the earlier works of Kehoe and Levine [124, 125], Kocherlakota [135], Alvarez and Jermann [12], and others on debt-constrained asset markets. In these models, the inability of agents to share risk perfectly and to fully offset the effects of idiosyncratic shocks leads to lower cross-country correlations of consumption and higher cross-country correlations of output. Kehoe and Perri [126] consider a standard international RBC model with production and capital accumulation. Output in each country is produced using capital and labor according to the constant-returns-to-scale production function:

$$F(k_i(s^{t-1}), A_i(s^t)l_i(s^t)),$$

where $A_i(s^t)$ is a random shock. The preferences of the representative consumer in each country are given by

$$\sum_{t=0}^{\infty} \sum_{s^t} \pi(s^t) U(c_i(s^t), l_i(s^t)),$$

where $c_i(s^t)$ denotes consumption of residents of country i. Under *complete markets*, the competitive equilibrium allocations solve the social planner's problem defined as

$$\sum_{t=0}^{\infty} \sum_{s^t} \pi(s^t)\beta^t \left[\phi_1 U(c_1(s^t), l_1(s^t)) + \phi_2 U(c_2(s^t), l_2(s^t)) \right], \qquad (2.23)$$

subject to the resource constraints

$$\sum_{i-1,2} \left[c_i(s^t) + k_i(s^t) \right] =$$

$$\sum_{i=1}^{2} \left[F(k_i(s^{t-1}), A_i(s^t)l_i(s^t)) + (1-\delta)k_i(s^{t-1}) \right]. \qquad (2.24)$$

The innovation in Kehoe and Perri [126] is to formulate a version of this problem that allows for *enforcement constraints*. These require that each country prefers the allocation it receives to the one that it could attain if it were in (financial) autarky from then onwards. The enforcement constraints are expressed as

$$\sum_{r=t}^{\infty} \sum_{s^r} \beta^{r-t}\pi(s^r|s^t)U(c_i(s^r), l_i(s^r)) \geq V_i(k_i(s^{t-1}), s^t), \qquad (2.25)$$

where $\pi(s^r|s^t)$ denotes the conditional probability of the history s^r given s^t and $V_i(k_i(s^{t-1}), s^t)$ denotes the value of autarky from s^t onwards, where $V_i(k_i(s^{t-1}), s^t)$ involves choosing $k_i(s^r), l_i(s^r), c_i(s^r)$ for $r \geq t$ to solve

$$V_i(k_i(s^{t-1}), s^t) = \max \sum_{r=t}^{\infty} \sum_{s^r} \beta^r \pi(s^r|s^t)U(c_i(s^r), l_i(s^r))$$

subject to

$$c_i(s^r) + k_i(s^r) \leq F(k_i(s^{r-1}), A_i(s^r)l_i(s^r)) + (1-\delta)k_i(s^{r-1}), \qquad r \geq t$$

given $k_i(s^{t-1})$.

As Kehoe and Perri [126] explain, the social planner's problem with enforcement constraints cannot be formulated recursively as a dynamic programming problem. The reason is that future decision variables such as $c_i(s^r)$ and $l_i(s^r)$ for $r > t$ enter the current enforcement constraints. An alternative approach involves adding a new pseudo state variable to achieve a recursive formulation of the original problem.[2] This approach is implemented by defining $\beta^t \pi(s^t)\mu_i(s^t)$ as the Lagrange multiplier on the enforcement constraints. The Lagrangian function becomes comprised of three terms: the weighted sum of utilities defined in (2.23), the standard resource constraints defined by (2.24), plus the term

$$\beta^t \pi(s^t)\mu_i(s^t)\left[\sum_{r=t}^{\infty}\sum_{s^r}\beta^{r-t}\pi(s^r|s^t)U(c_i(s^r),l_i(s^r)) - V_i(k_i(s^{t-1}),s^t)\right].$$

Since $\pi(s^r) = \pi(s^r|s^t)\pi(s^t)$, the Lagrangian function is written as

$$\sum_{t=0}^{\infty}\sum_{s^t}\sum_{i}\beta^t\pi(s^t)\left[M_i(s^{t-1})U(c_i(s^t),l_i(s^t))\right.$$
$$\left. + \mu_i(s^t)[U(c_i(s^t),l_i(s^t)) - V_i(k_i(s^{t-1}),s^t)]\right]$$

plus the terms relating to the resource constraints. In this expression, $M_i(s^{t-1})$ satisfies

$$M_i(s^t) = M_i(s^{t-1}) + \mu_i(s^t), \quad t \geq 0$$

with $M_i(s^{t-1}) = \phi_i$. Thus, $M_i(s^t)$ are just the original planning weights plus the sum of the multipliers $\mu_i(s^t)$ along the path s^t.

It is beyond the scope of this book to derive a solution for the model with enforcement constraints. Therefore, we will focus on the results of simulating this model and compare it with alternatives that have been obtained in the literature. Kehoe and Perri [126] generate solutions for three different economies: complete markets, a bond economy, and an economy with enforcement constraints. The bond economy stipulates that all intertemporal trades must be implemented with an uncontingent bond. Thus, the budget constraints for households in each country are expressed as

$$c_i(s^t) + k_i(s^t) + q(s^t)b_i(s^t) \leq w_i(s^t)l_i(s^t)$$
$$+ [r_i(s^t) + (1 - \delta)]k_i(s^{t-1}) + b_i(s^{t-1}),$$

---

[2]For other applications, see Marcet and Marimon [155].

where $w_i(s^t)$ and $r_i(s^t)$ denote the wage rate and the rental rate on capital in country i, $q(s^t)$ is the period t price of an uncontingent that pays off one unit in period $t + 1$ regardless of the state, and $b_i(s^t)$ is the quantity of the bond by consumers in country i. There is also a borrowing constraint that requires that borrowing cannot exceed some finite bound, $b(s^t) \geq -\bar{b}$, where $0 < \bar{b} < \infty$. Preferences in each country are taken to be of the form

$$U(c, l) = \frac{\left(c^\gamma(1 - l)^{1-\gamma}\right)^{1-\sigma}}{1 - \sigma}, \quad 0 < \gamma < 1, \quad \sigma \geq 0, \quad (2.26)$$

and the production function as

$$F(k, AL) = k^\alpha (AL)^{1-\alpha}, \quad 0 < \alpha < 1. \quad (2.27)$$

The parameter values that are considered are standard, and given by $\beta = 0.99, \gamma = 0.36, \sigma = 2, \alpha = 0.36$, and $\delta = 0.025$. The coefficients of the A matrix, which governs the persistence properties of the shocks and the spillovers between them, are parameterized in different ways. According to one parameterization intended to capture substantial *persistence*, the autoregressive coefficients of the shocks for each country captured by the diagonal elements of the A matrix are set at 0.9 and the off-diagonal elements are set at zero. These values are consistent with those assumed by Kollman [136] and Baxter and Crucini [34]. A second parameterization allows for *high persistence* with the diagonal elements equal to 0.99 and the off-diagonal elements equal to zero, and a third one allows for *high spillover* with the diagonal elements equal to 0.85 and the off-diagonal elements equal to 0.15. Similar to Backus *et al.* [25], the variance of the innovations to the productivity shocks in each country is set at $Var(\epsilon_{i,t}) = 0.007$ and the correlation of the shocks is set at 0.25.

The findings from the model echo many of the earlier findings. Under the *complete markets* specification, the model displays many of the anomalies reported in the literature. First, the consumption correlations are significantly higher than the output correlations in the model, whereas these correlations are the opposite in the data. Second, the cross-country correlations of employment and investment are negative in the model, whereas they are positive in the data. Third, net exports and investment are much more volatile in the model than they are in the data. In the *bond economy*, the three discrepancies between the model and the data remain, albeit with some minor improvements in the various statistics. In the economy with *enforcement constraints*, the output and consumption correlations are both positive and closer to each other, although the cross-country correlation of consumption is greater than that of output. Second, the cross-country correlations of employment and investment have now switched from being negative to positive; and third, the volatility of net exports and investment has declined dramatically. The only remaining discrepancy is that net exports are procyclical in the model whereas they are countercyclical in the data.

As discussed earlier, the frictionless international RBC model implies that investment flows to the country with the higher productivity shock, leading to very volatile investment and net exports. In the literature, exogenous adjustment costs are typically added to inhibit the flow of investment. Kehoe and Perri [126] note that the enforcement constraint acts as an endogenous inhibiting factor. Considering economies with exogenous adjustment costs to investment, they find that the volatilities of investment and net exports are diminished, but that the anomalies regarding the cross-correlations of output, consumption, investment, and employment remain. Finally, the authors examine the response of the variables in domestic and foreign countries to a positive shock to productivity in the domestic country. This increases the productivity of both capital and labor in the domestic country, so resources are optimally shifted there. The capital stock in the domestic country increases, as domestic residents save more and also as investment from abroad flows there. The net flow of investment increases the trade deficit in the domestic country. In the foreign country, we notice declines in employment and investment. Thus, we see that the differing responses of the domestic versus the foreign country lead to the negative cross-country correlations of employment and investment. Since residents of each country can acquire contingent claims that allow them to smooth consumption across all possible history of shocks, risk sharing across countries implies that consumption increases in the foreign country. Consumption increases substantially more in the domestic country because consumption and labor complement each other. Hence, we observe the high cross-country correlations between domestic and foreign consumption. In the bond economy, the responses are similar to those for the complete markets economy, but because of restrictions on asset trading, they are somewhat dampened.

Finally, let us consider the impact of a positive productivity shock in the enforcement economy. Suppose that the social planner tries to implement the complete markets allocation for this economy. The high and persistent productivity shock in the domestic country increases the value of autarky, increasing the incentives for default. The increased investment flows to the domestic country further increase the value of autarky. Hence, the planner must restrict investment to the domestic country to prevent the default option from being exercised. Furthermore, the planner also builds up the capital stock in the foreign country to ensure that the risk-sharing arrangement between the domestic and foreign countries is not reneged upon. In terms of the behavior of consumption, the complete markets allocation implies that an increase in output in the domestic country will lead to increases in consumption in both the domestic and foreign countries. In the presence of an enforcement constraint, however, this is not possible. Hence, to ensure that domestic country residents consume more than foreign country residents, the social planner increases the relative weight on the utility of domestic country residents (recall that the social planner's weight is the inverse of the marginal utility of consumption). Over time, as the productivity shock dies out, the value of autarky diminishes and the relative weight on the home country also falls.

4.3. OTHER EXTENSIONS

The international RBC literature has sought to reconcile the findings in the data not only in terms of the cross-country consumption correlations, but also for the behavior of output, investment, and the real exchange rate. As a result, models that relax assumptions regarding preferences, the production side, and the presence of additional shocks have been developed. We describe a few of these extensions in what follows.

Hess and Shin [119] re-explore the two international business cycle anomalies emphasized by Backus *et al.* [25] as well as establish the pattern of productivity growth between industries and countries. They then compare these findings for the international business cycle to those obtained for data between regions within a country — the so-called "intranational business cycle". They argue that the intranational business cycle is a natural environment for thinking about the interactions between economies when there are no trade frictions and when there are not multiple currencies. Ambler *et al.* [13] modify the supply side of a two-country model by adding multiple sectors and trade in intermediate goods. The model generates a higher cross-country correlation of output than standard one-sector models. It also predicts cross-country correlations of employment and investment that are closer to the data.

Stockman and Tesar [200] introduce a nontraded goods sector in each country. Similar to our discussion above, they argue that introducing nontraded goods may be a way of re-establishing the link between a nation's output and its spending. They employ preferences that depend on consumption of the tradable goods of countries 1 and 2, a nontradable good, and leisure. Preferences are assumed to be nonseparable with respect to a composite good, consisting of the tradable goods of countries 1 and 2, and a nontradable good. In their model, output in the traded and nontraded goods sector of each country is produced using sector-specific capital and labor which is mobile between sectors. However, there is no international capital or labor mobility. The authors find that the model predicts the correlation between home and foreign output, overstates the cross-country correlation of aggregate consumption, and greatly overstates the cross-country correlation of tradable consumption. Hence, they find that introducing nontradable goods does not suffice to reduce the cross-country correlation of consumption. Likewise, they find that the model overstates the negative correlation between the relative price of nontradable to tradable goods and relative consumption of nontraded to traded goods, and understates the variability of the trade balance. They conclude that an international business cycle model driven solely by productivity shocks cannot account for the findings. Instead, they argue that what is needed is a source of nation-specific shocks that shift *demand*. They introduce taste shocks that affect the utility of traded versus nontraded goods and find that this feature brings the data more in line with the implications of the model.

Baxter and Farr [35] develop a model with variable capital utilization as a way of accounting for the international correlations. They argue that variable capacity utilization has the potential to account for the co-movement of factor inputs across countries. We already considered the role of variable factor utilization in reconciling the behavior of procyclical productivity in closed-economy business cycle models (see also Burnside and Eichenbaum [51], Basu [29], or Basu and Kimball [30]). The notion is that a positive shock to productivity in the domestic country will tend to reduce the investment flow across countries by leading to an increase in capital utilization rather than investment. As we described above, many of the puzzles of the international business cycle literature can be addressed successfully by devising a mechanism to limit investment flows across borders. Kehoe and Perri [126] achieve this through an enforcement constraint which requires that the utility under the constrained allocation exceed the utility that country could obtain under autarky after defaulting on its international debt obligations.

Baxter and Farr [35] assume that preferences are given by the specification in equation (2.26). Output in the domestic country is produced using capital services S_t and labor L_t as

$$Y_t = A_t S_t^{1-\alpha}(X_t L_t)^\alpha, \quad 0 < \alpha < 1,$$

where capital services are the product of the capital stock, K_t, and the utilization rate, Z_t:

$$S_t = Z_t K_t.$$

The capital accumulation process displays both costly utilization of capital and adjustment costs:

$$K_{t+1} = [1 - \delta(Z_t)] + \phi(I_t/K_t)K_t,$$

where $\delta' > 0$, $\delta'' > 0$, $\phi' > 0$, and $\phi'' < 0$. Similar functions characterize the foreign country. International trade in assets is made solely with one-period, real pure discount bonds which have the price $q_t = [1 + r_t]^{-1}$. Assuming that the household in each country owns the capital stock and makes real investment decisions, the budget constraint for the representative household is given by

$$C_t + I_t + q_t B_{t+1} \le Y_t + B_t,$$

where B_{t+1} is the quantity of bonds carried over into the next period.

The parameterization of the capital utilization function and the adjustment cost function are key aspects of the quantitative analysis. The covariance properties of the technology processes for the domestic and foreign technology shocks are parameterized to be near unit roots with zero spillover effects. The correlation of the innovations to the technology shocks is set at 0.258, which is consistent with earlier studies. Finally, the variance of the innovations is set so that the variance of output in the model exactly matches the volatility of the US economy. One of the key findings regarding the role of variable capital utilization is that, first, the volatility of the shocks necessary to match output volatility is substantially reduced. Second, introducing variable capital utilization reduces the volatilities of consumption, capital, and exports, which is desirable, and also those of hours and employment, which is not. The most important impact of variable factor utilization is on the cross-correlations of the factor inputs. Specifically, the cross-correlation of hours and investment become positive. Intuitively, variable capital utilization takes the place of investment flows across countries. When a positive productivity shock occurs in one country, capital utilization rates increase, which in turn increase employment. Even with a modest cross-country correlation of the innovations, this is accompanied by increases in investment and employment in the other country.

4.4. PUZZLES REVISITED

The puzzles in the international business cycle literature have been the topic of much research (see, for example, the survey by Baxter [33]). In their review, Obstfeld and Rogoff [168] argue that many of the puzzles in international macroeconomics may just be specific to the models researchers are using. In our earlier discussion, we described the puzzles that arose when trying to match the international RBC model to the data. Obstfeld and Rogoff [168] provide a broader view of the empirical puzzles in the international macroeconomics literature, though they also relate their discussion to the international RBC literature. They enumerate the following discrepancies between data and existing theory as "puzzles":

- **Home bias in trade**: A number of authors have documented that *intranational* trade is typically much greater than *international* trade. See, for example, McCallum [157] or Helliwell [118].
- **The Feldstein–Horioka puzzle**: According to this puzzle, long averages of saving rates and investment rates tend to be correlated for the OECD countries (see Feldstein and Horioka [89]). Yet, in a world of integrated capital markets, we would expect capital to flow to regions where the rates of return are highest.

- **Home bias in equity portfolios**: This reflects the puzzling preference of stock market investors for home assets (for a recent elaboration, see Tesar and Werner [203]). In Section 4.2, we discussed various explanations that account for this puzzle — the presence of human capital as discussed by Baxter and Jermann [36] or nontraded goods.

- **The international consumption correlation puzzle**: We already discussed the finding that cross-country consumption correlations exceed the cross-country output correlations in a typical international RBC model, whereas the opposite is true in the data. Backus and Smith [24] show that in an economy with traded and nontraded goods, perfect risk sharing across countries implies that countries which experience declines in the relative price of consumption should receive large transfers of goods.

- **The purchasing power parity (PPP) puzzle**: The PPP puzzle arises from the fact that shocks to the real exchange rate are very persistent.

- **The exchange rate disconnect puzzle**: This puzzle captures the notion that there exists a relationship between exchange rates and *any* macroeconomic variable. Meese and Rogoff [161] further show that most exchange rate models forecast exchange rates no better than a naive random walk.

Surprisingly, Obstfeld and Rogoff [168] find that adding transport costs goes a long way towards accounting for the first five puzzles. They argue that, first, the international consumption correlation puzzle tends to be specific to a model's assumptions, as we described above, and does not have the same weight as, say, the international portfolio diversification puzzle. Second, the last two puzzles are pricing puzzles, whereas the other four refer to the behavior of quantities. They also note that the pricing puzzles require such features as nominal rigidities of the type that we will consider in the next chapter. In contrast to some of the other contributions that we have discussed, the analysis of Obstfeld and Rogoff [168] is an attempt to unify the explanations of a related but disparate set of findings. Clearly, the literature that we have described has revealed a variety of promising directions for future research.

Chapter 5

New Keynesian Models

The New Keynesian approach has gained significance in the modern macroeconomics literature. Critics of the original real business cycle (RBC) approach had, from the onset, taken issue with the notion that prices can adjust costlessly to clear markets. More recently, New Keynesian theories have revived interest in business cycle models that are capable of producing short-run economic fluctuations based on the types of forces that Keynes had initially postulated. Prototypical New Keynesian models such as that by Rotemberg and Woodford [182] allow for imperfect competition and markups to capture alternative propagation mechanisms in response to technology shocks or shocks to government expenditures. Limited participation models also allow alternative mechanisms for the propagation of real and monetary shocks.[1]

The behavior of hours and productivity has been a topic of debate. The RBC conclusions regarding the response of hours, output, and other variables to a technology shock have been questioned by empirical results obtained along several different lines. On the one hand, Gali [96] has argued that in a suitably restricted vector autoregression (VAR) including measures of hours, productivity, output, and other variables, the response of hours to productivity shocks is negative. This is in contrast to the RBC model, which predicts that hours rise on impact to a positive technology shock. Basu, Fernald, and Kimball [32] also present evidence that hours worked and other variables fall in response to technology improvements in the short run. Their approach involves purging the standard Solow residual of factors that might lead to procyclicality, such as variable factor utilization. There also exist open-economy versions of the New Keynesian model that have been used for policy analysis

---

[1] For a review and discussion of these models, see Christiano, Eichenbaum, and Evans [66].

and for understanding the role of monetary shocks.[2] We first describe a simple New Keynesian framework that can be used to rationalize the observations, and then discuss the empirical findings in more detail.

5.1. THE BASIC MODEL

Consider a simple New Keynesian model with monopolistic competition, price rigidities, and variable labor effort due to Gali [96]. Suppose that a representative household chooses consumption C_t, money holdings M_t, hours worked N_t, and effort levels U_t to maximize

$$E_0 \left\{ \sum_{t=0}^{\infty} \beta^t \left[\ln(C_t) + \lambda_m \ln \left(\frac{M_t}{P_t} \right) - H(N_t, U_t) \right] \right\} \quad (1.1)$$

subject to

$$\int_0^1 P_{it} C_{it} di + M_t = W_t N_t + V_t U_t + M_{t-1} + \Upsilon_t + \Pi_t \quad (1.2)$$

for $t = 0, 1, 2, \ldots$. In this expression, C_t is a composite consumption good defined as

$$C_t = \left(\int_0^1 C_{it}^{(\epsilon-1)/\epsilon} di \right)^{\epsilon/(\epsilon-1)}, \quad (1.3)$$

where C_{it} is the quantity of good $i \in [0, 1]$ consumed in period t, and $\epsilon > 1$ is the elasticity of substitution among consumption goods. The price of good i is given by P_{it}, and

$$P_t = \left(\int_0^1 P_{it}^{1-\epsilon} di \right)^{1/(1-\epsilon)} \quad (1.4)$$

is the aggregate price index. The functional form for $H(N_t, U_t)$ is given by

$$H(N_t, U_t) = \frac{\lambda_n}{1 + \sigma_n} N_t^{1+\sigma_n} + \frac{\lambda_u}{1 + \sigma_u} U_t^{1+\sigma_u}. \quad (1.5)$$

Υ_t and Π_t denote monetary transfers and profits, respectively. W_t and V_t denote the nominal prices of an hour of work and effort, respectively.

---

[2] For a further discussion, see Bowman and Doyle [45].

The first-order conditions with respect to the household's problem are given by

$$\mu_t P_{it} = \frac{1}{C_t} \left(\int_0^1 C_{it}^{(\epsilon-1)/\epsilon} di \right)^{1/(\epsilon-1)} C_{it}^{-1/\epsilon}, \quad i \in [0,1], \quad (1.6)$$

$$\lambda_m \frac{1}{M_t} = \mu_t - \beta E_t(\mu_{t+1}), \quad (1.7)$$

$$\lambda_n N_t^{\sigma_n} = \mu_t W_t, \quad (1.8)$$

$$\lambda_u U_t^{\sigma_u} = \mu_t V_t, \quad (1.9)$$

where μ_t denotes the Lagrange multiplier on the period-by-period budget constraint. We can solve for μ_t from the first-order condition corresponding to the consumption choice as $\mu_t = 1/(P_t C_t)$. Substituting for this variable and simplifying yields

$$C_{it} = \left(\frac{P_{it}}{P_t} \right)^{-\epsilon} C_t, \quad i \in [0,1], \quad (1.10)$$

$$\frac{1}{C_t} = \lambda_m \frac{P_t}{M_t} + \beta E_t \left(\frac{1}{C_{t+1}} \frac{P_t}{P_{t+1}} \right), \quad (1.11)$$

$$\lambda_n N_t^{\sigma_n} C_t = \frac{W_t}{P_t}, \quad (1.12)$$

$$\lambda_u U_t^{\sigma_u} C_t = \frac{V_t}{P_t}. \quad (1.13)$$

In this economy, good i is produced by firm i using the production function

$$Y_{it} = Z_t L_{it}^{\alpha}, \quad (1.14)$$

where L_{it} is the quantity of effective labor used by firm i:

$$L_{it} = N_{it}^{\theta} U_{it}^{1-\theta}, \quad 0 < \theta < 1. \quad (1.15)$$

Z_t is an aggregate technology shock whose growth rate follows an i.i.d. process $\{\eta_t\}$ with $\eta_t \sim N(0, \sigma_\eta^2)$:

$$Z_t = Z_{t-1} \exp(\eta_t). \quad (1.16)$$

Consider first the choice of optimal inputs of hours and effort chosen by the firm to minimize its costs subject to the production technology. Let λ be the

Lagrange multiplier on the technology constraint. The first-order conditions are given by

$$W_t = \lambda Z_t \theta \alpha N_{it}^{\theta\alpha-1} U_{it}^{(1-\theta)\alpha}, \tag{1.17}$$

$$V_t = \lambda Z_t (1-\theta)\alpha N_{it}^{\theta\alpha} U_{it}^{(1-\theta)\alpha-1}. \tag{1.18}$$

The ratio of these conditions yields

$$\frac{\theta}{1-\theta} \frac{U_{it}}{N_{it}} = \frac{W_t}{V_t}. \tag{1.19}$$

Notice that the firm will be willing to accommodate any changes in demand at the given price P_{it} as long as this price is above marginal cost. Hence, the firm chooses the output level

$$Y_{it} = \left(\frac{P_{it}}{P_t}\right)^{-\epsilon} C_t. \tag{1.20}$$

Thus, when choosing price, the firm will solve the problem

$$\max_{P_{it}} E_{t-1}\{(1/C_t)(P_{it}Y_{it} - W_t N_{it} - V_t U_{it})\} \tag{1.21}$$

subject to (1.19) and (1.20). To find the first-order condition for this problem, we will use the last two constraints to solve for the firm's cost function as

$$W_t N_{it} + V_t U_{it} = W_t N_{it} + \frac{1-\theta}{\theta} \frac{W_t}{V_t} V_t N_{it}$$

$$= \frac{W_t N_{it}}{\theta} = \frac{W_t Y_{it}^{1/\alpha}}{\theta Z_t^{1/\alpha}((1-\theta)W_t/\theta V_t)^{1-\theta}}$$

$$= \frac{W_t (P_{it}/P_t)^{-\epsilon/\alpha} C_t^{1/\alpha}}{\theta Z_t^{1/\alpha}((1-\theta)W_t/\theta V_t)^{1-\theta}}.$$

Using this result, the first-order condition is

$$E_{t-1}\left\{(1/C_t)\left(\alpha\theta P_{it}Y_{it} - \frac{\epsilon}{\epsilon-1}W_t N_{it}\right)\right\} = 0. \tag{1.22}$$

Finally, the quantity of money is determined as

$$M_t^s = M_{t-1}^s \exp(\xi_t + \gamma\eta_t), \tag{1.23}$$

where $\{\xi_t\}$ is a white noise that is orthogonal to $\{\eta_t\}$, with $\xi_t \sim N(0, \sigma_m^2)$.

In a *symmetric equilibrium*, all firms charge the same price P_t and choose the same levels of the inputs and output N_t, U_t, and Y_t. Market clearing in the goods market requires that $C_t = C_{it} = Y_{it} = Y_t$. Finally, equilibrium in the money market requires that the growth rate of the money stock evolve exogenously as $M_t/M_{t-1} = \exp(\xi_t + \gamma\eta_t)$.

Next, assume that consumption is proportional to real balances in equilibrium, $C_t = M_t/P_t$. This, together with market-clearing conditions, implies that $P_t Y_t = M_t$. Using the first-order condition for consumption in (1.11) and the money growth rule in (1.23) yields

$$C_t = \lambda_m^{-1}\frac{M_t}{P_t}\left[1 - \beta E_t\left(\frac{P_t}{P_{t+1}}\frac{Y_t}{Y_{t+1}}\right)\right]$$

$$= \lambda_m^{-1}\frac{M_t}{P_t}\left[1 - \beta\exp(\sigma_m^2 + \gamma^2\sigma_\eta^2)/2\right]$$

$$= \Phi\frac{M_t}{P_t}, \tag{1.24}$$

where $\Phi = \lambda_m^{-1}[1 - \beta\exp(\sigma_m^2 + \gamma^2\sigma_\eta^2)/2]$. Next, use (1.12), (1.13), and (1.19). Taking the ratio of the first two conditions yields

$$\frac{W_t}{V_t} = \frac{\lambda_n}{\lambda_u}\frac{N_t^{\sigma_n}}{U_t^{\sigma_u}}.$$

Equating this with (1.19) yields

$$\frac{U_t}{N_t} = \frac{1-\theta}{\theta}\frac{\lambda_n}{\lambda_u}\frac{N_t^{\sigma_n}}{U_t^{\sigma_u}}.$$

Solving for U_t yields

$$U_t = A^{1/\alpha(1-\theta)}N_t^{(1+\sigma_n)/(1+\sigma_u)}, \tag{1.25}$$

where $A = ((1-\theta)/\theta(\lambda_n/\lambda_u))^{\alpha(1-\theta)/(1+\sigma_u)}$. Substituting this result into the equation for the production function yields

$$Y_t = AZ_t N_t^\varphi, \tag{1.26}$$

where $\varphi = \alpha\theta + (1+\sigma_n)\alpha(1-\theta)/(1+\sigma_u)$. Using the price-setting rule in (1.22) together with (1.12) and the expression for equilibrium consumption and output derived above, we can show that

$$\Delta p_t = \xi_{t-1} - (1-\gamma)\eta_{t-1}, \tag{1.27}$$

$$\Delta y_t = \Delta \xi_t + \gamma \eta_t + (1-\gamma)\eta_{t-1}, \tag{1.28}$$

$$n_t = \frac{1}{\varphi}\xi_t - \frac{1-\gamma}{\varphi}\eta_t, \tag{1.29}$$

$$\Delta x_t = \left(1 - \frac{1}{\varphi}\right)\Delta \xi_t + \left(\frac{1-\gamma}{\varphi} + \gamma\right)\eta_t$$

$$+ (1-\gamma)\left(1 - \frac{1}{\varphi}\right)\eta_{t-1}, \tag{1.30}$$

where $x = y - n$ is the log of labor productivity.

The conditions in (1.27)–(1.30) can be used to describe the impact of monetary versus technology shocks. A positive *monetary shock* defined by $\xi_t > 0$ has a temporary impact on output, employment, and productivity. This can be observed by noting that the levels of y_t, n_t, and x_t depend only on the current ξ_t. Hence, an increase in ξ_t causes output and employment to go up for one period and then to revert back to their initial values. The impact of ξ_t on labor productivity is also transitory, but the sign depends on whether $\varphi < (>)1$. We note that measured labor productivity responds positively whenever $\varphi > 1$, which corresponds to the situation of short-run increasing returns to labor. Finally, the price level responds one-for-one to an increase in ξ_t, though with a one-period lag.

A positive *technology shock* defined by $\eta_t > 0$ has a permanent positive one-for-one impact on output and productivity and a permanent negative impact on the price level if $\gamma < 1$. More interestingly, a positive technology shock has a *negative* short-run impact on employment. This result can be best understood by considering the case of $\gamma = 0$, that is, when there is no accommodating response in the money supply to real shocks. In such a case, given a constant money supply and predetermined prices, real balances remain unchanged in the face of a positive technology shock. Hence, demand remains unchanged so that firms will be able to meet demand by producing an unchanged level of output. However, with a positive shock to technology, producing the same output will require less labor input, and hence a decline in employment will occur.

5.2. EMPIRICAL EVIDENCE

Gali [96] estimates a structural VAR (SVAR) and identifies technology shocks as the only shocks that are allowed to have a permanent effect on average labor productivity. This is similar to the approach in Blanchard and Quah [43] for identifying demand versus supply shocks using long-run restrictions on estimated VARs. The SVAR model interprets the behavior of (log) hours n_t and (log) productivity x_t in terms of two types of exogenous disturbances — technology and non-technology shocks — which are orthogonal to each other and whose impact is propagated through time based on some unspecified mechanisms as

$$\begin{bmatrix} \Delta x_t \\ \Delta n_t \end{bmatrix} = \begin{bmatrix} C^{11}(L) & C^{12}(L) \\ C^{21}(L) & C^{22}(L) \end{bmatrix} \begin{bmatrix} \epsilon_t^z \\ \epsilon_t^m \end{bmatrix} = C(L)\epsilon_t,$$

where ϵ_t^z and ϵ_t^m denote the sequences of technology and non-technology shocks, respectively. The orthogonality assumption, together with a normalization, implies that $E(\epsilon_t \epsilon_t') = I$. The identifying assumption is that only technology shocks have a permanent effect on productivity, which can be expressed as the restriction $C^{12}(1) = 0$.[3] Gali [96] estimates this model using postwar US data. Surprisingly, he finds that alternative measures of labor input *decline* in response to a positive technology shock while GDP adjusts only gradually to its long-run level. Furthermore, technology shocks explain only a small fraction of employment and output fluctuations. By contrast, Gali [96] finds that variables that have no permanent effects on employment (and which are referred to as demand shocks) explain a substantial fraction of the variation in both employment and output. Christiano, Eichenbaum, and Vigfusson [68] suggest that the standard RBC results hold if per capita hours are measured in log-levels as opposed to differences.

Chari, Kehoe, and McGrattan [63] have challenged the findings derived from so-called SVARs. First, they argue that the difference specification for aggregate hours is *a priori* misspecified because all RBC models imply that per capita hours is a stationary variable. Second, they argue that if the simulated data from a simple RBC model are subjected to a SVAR-based test, the difference-stationary version of the model implies that the response

---

[3]The value of the matrix $C(L)$ evaluated at $L = 1$ gives the long-run multipliers for the model, i.e., the long-run impact of a given shock.

of hours to a shock to productivity is negative as in Gali and Rabanal [98]. However, if hours worked is considered to be stationary in levels, then they argue that the confidence bands for the impulse response functions from the SVAR are so wide that the procedure is uninformative about the question at hand. They trace the source of the difference to the failure to include a sufficient number of lags in the estimated VAR specifications so as to adequately capture the behavior of hours implied by the underlying theoretical model. This misspecification, in their view, leads to an erroneous conclusion of the negative response of hours worked to a productivity shock, even though the data underlying this test are drawn from a standard RBC model which implies the opposite response!

Despite the controversies surrounding the SVAR approach, Basu *et al.* [32] present evidence that support the SVAR findings by generating a modified Solow residual that accounts for imperfect competition, non-constant returns to scale, variable factor utilization, and sectoral re-allocation and aggregation effects. Unlike the SVAR approach, the evidence obtained from this approach is robust to long-run identifying assumptions or to the inclusion of new variables in the estimated dynamic system. They find that purging the standard Solow residual of these effects eliminates the phenomenon of "procyclical productivity". They also examine the response of a key set of variables such as output, hours worked, utilization, employment, non-residential investment, durables and residential investment, non-durables and services, and various prices and interest rates to changes in the purified Solow residual. They use both standard regression analysis and simple bivariate VARs for this purpose. Their findings corroborate the findings from the SVAR approach regarding the negative response of hours to technology improvements in the short run. They also uncover further evidence for the negative response of non-residential investment to such shocks. Following Gali [96] and Gali and Rabanal [98], they advance price rigidity as the major reason for these deviations from the RBC predictions in the short run. These findings have, on the one hand, generated substantial controversy and, on the other, cast further doubt on the ability of the RBC model driven by technology shocks to provide a convincing explanation of economic fluctuations for the major developed countries.

Chapter 6
Business Cycles in Emerging Market Economies

In recent years, the real business cycle (RBC) agenda has been increasingly applied in emerging market contexts. On the one hand, researchers have begun generating business cycle facts for such economies (see, for example, Ratfai and Benczur [175, 176]). On the other hand, they have been examining the efficacy of RBC-type models in accounting for these facts. Business cycles in emerging markets exhibit different characteristics compared to those in developed economies. The recent literature on the "Sudden Stop" phenomenon has emphasized the large reversals in current accounts and the incidence of capital outflows that have become identified with many recent emerging market economies' experience (see, for example, Arellano and Mendoza [17]). Emerging market business cycles also display a different set of stylized facts relative to developed economies. For instance, consumption varies more than output, the trade balance is strongly countercyclical, and income and exports are typically highly volatile. The question then arises whether a small open economy-type RBC model can account for both developed and emerging market business cycles.

Earlier RBC models for small open economies were developed by Mendoza [162] and Correia, Neves, and Rebelo [77]. Kydland and Zaragaza [144] also study the behavior of an emerging market economy, namely, Argentina, but their analysis is based on the one-sector optimal growth model. They argue that the large shortfalls in GDP suffered by Argentina in the 1980s can be explained in a simple growth model framework using the observed measure of productivity or the Solow residual. More recently, Aguiar and Gopinath

[1] and Garcia-Cicco, Pancrazi, and Uribe [101] have examined versions of a small open-economy business cycle model with permanent and transitory shocks to account for emerging versus developed economy experiences.

6.1. A SMALL OPEN-ECONOMY MODEL OF EMERGING MARKET BUSINESS CYCLES

Aguiar and Gopinath [1] present a small open-economy model of business cycles that allows for permanent and transitory changes to productivity. In their view, emerging market economies' experience can be distinguished by the large number of regime shifts, here modeled as changes in trend productivity growth. By contrast, developed economies typically face stable political and economic policy regimes so that changes to productivity are transitory.

To describe the model, let output be produced according to the Cobb–Douglas production technology as

$$Y_t = \exp(z_t) K_t^{1-\alpha} (\Gamma_t L_t)^{\alpha}, \quad 0 < \alpha < 1, \tag{1.1}$$

where $\{z_t\}$ and $\{\Gamma_t\}$ represent two alternative productivity processes. The shock z_t represents the *transitory* component of productivity, and evolves as a stationary AR(1) process:

$$z_t = \rho_z z_{t-1} + \epsilon_t^z, \quad |\rho_z| < 1, \tag{1.2}$$

where $\{\epsilon_t^z\}_{t=0}^{\infty}$ is distributed as i.i.d. with $E(\epsilon_t^z) = 0$ and $Var(\epsilon_t^z) = \sigma_z^2$.

The *permanent* shock to productivity evolves as

$$\Gamma_t = g_t \Gamma_{t-1} = \prod_{s=0}^{t} g_s, \tag{1.3}$$

$$\ln(g_t) = (1 - \rho_g) \ln(\mu_g) + \rho_g \ln(g_{t-1}) + \epsilon_t^g, \quad |\rho_g| < 1, \tag{1.4}$$

where $\{\epsilon_t^g\}_{t=0}^{\infty}$ is distributed as i.i.d. with $E(\epsilon_t^g) = 0$ and $Var(\epsilon_t^g) = \sigma_g^2$. Thus, g_t denotes the shocks to the growth rate of productivity, and μ_g denotes average long-run productivity growth. Since productivity and output depend on the cumulation of the shocks g_t, a stationarity-inducing transformation is used to remove the stochastic trend from all variables as

$$\hat{x}_t = \frac{x_t}{\Gamma_{t-1}}.$$

Aguiar and Gopinath [1] consider two types of preferences over consumption and leisure. The first is from the class of so-called GHH (after Greenwood, Hercowitz, and Huffman [105]) and the second are standard Cobb–Douglas preferences. The GHH preferences are defined as

$$u_t = \frac{(C_t - \tau \Gamma_{t-1} L_t^{\nu})^{1-\sigma}}{1 - \sigma}, \quad \nu > 1, \ \tau > 0. \tag{1.5}$$

Here, the elasticity of labor supply is given by $1/(\nu - 1)$, and the intertemporal elasticity of substitution is given by $1/\sigma$. In the Cobb–Douglas case, preferences are given by

$$u_t = \frac{(C_t^{\gamma}(1 - L_t)^{1-\gamma})^{1-\sigma}}{1 - \sigma}, \quad 0 < \gamma < 1, \ \sigma \geq 0. \tag{1.6}$$

The expected discounted utility of the representative consumer can be written as

$$\frac{1}{1 - \sigma} E_0\{(C_0 - \tau L_0^{\nu})^{1-\sigma} + \beta \Gamma_0^{1-\sigma}(\hat{C}_1 - \tau L_1^{\nu})^{1-\sigma}$$

$$+ \beta^2 \Gamma_1^{1-\sigma}(\hat{C}_2 - \tau L_2^{\nu})^{1-\sigma} \ldots\}$$

$$= \frac{1}{1 - \sigma} E_0\{(C_0 - \tau L_0^{\nu})^{1-\sigma} + \beta g_0^{1-\sigma}(\hat{C}_1 - \tau L_1^{\nu})^{1-\sigma}$$

$$+ E_1\{\beta^2 g_0 g_1^{1-\sigma}(\hat{C}_2 - \tau L_2^{\nu})^{1-\sigma} \ldots\}\}$$

$$= \frac{1}{1 - \sigma} E_0\{(C_0 - \tau L_0^{\nu})^{1-\sigma} + \beta g_0^{1-\sigma}(\hat{C}_1 - \tau L_1^{\nu})^{1-\sigma}$$

$$+ \beta g_0 E_1\{\beta g_1^{1-\sigma}(\hat{C}_2 - \tau L_2^{\nu})^{1-\sigma} \ldots\}\},$$

where the last line is obtained by substituting recursively and making use of an iterated expectations argument. Thus, expected discounted utility remains bounded provided $\beta E(g_t) = \beta \mu_g < 1$.

The economy-wide resource constraint is given by

$$C_t + K_{t+1} = Y_t + (1 - \delta)K_t + \frac{\phi}{2}\left(\frac{K_{t+1}}{K_t} - \mu_g\right)^2 K_t - B_t + q_t B_{t+1}. \tag{1.7}$$

This shows that investment is subject to quadratic costs of adjustment, and that the country can borrow using one-period debt that sells for the price

q_t. The price of debt for the country depends on the quantity of debt outstanding as

$$\frac{1}{q_t} = 1 + r_t = 1 + r^* + \psi \left[\exp \left(\frac{B_{t+1}}{\Gamma_t} - b \right) - 1 \right], \qquad (1.8)$$

where r^* is the world interest rate, b represents the steady-state level of debt, and $\psi > 0$ governs the elasticity of the interest rate to changes in indebtedness. Furthermore, when choosing how much debt to take on, the individual country does not internalize the fact that an increase in borrowing will lead to an increase in the interest rate on those loans.

The model expressed in terms of the transformed or "hatted" variables is solved by using standard recursive methods. Assuming it exists, the value function defined in terms of the transformed variables is given by

$$V(\hat{K}_t, \hat{B}_t, z_t, g_t)$$
$$= \max_{\hat{C}_t, L_t, \hat{K}_{t+1}, \hat{B}_{t+1}} \{ u(\hat{C}_t, L_t) + f(\beta, g_t) E_t V(\hat{K}_{t+1}, \hat{B}_{t+1}, z_{t+1}, g_{t+1}) \},$$

where $u(\hat{C}_t, L_t)$ is defined by (1.5) in the case of GHH preferences and by (1.6) in the case of Cobb–Douglas preferences. Likewise, $f(\beta, g_t)$ is given by $\beta g_t^{1-\sigma}$ in the former case and by $\beta g_t^{\gamma(1-\sigma)}$ in the latter. The optimization is subject to the transformed budget constraint

$$\hat{C}_t + g_t \hat{K}_{t+1} = \hat{Y}_t + (1 - \delta)\hat{K}_t$$
$$- \frac{\phi}{2} \left(g_t \frac{\hat{K}_{t+1}}{\hat{K}_t} - \mu_g \right)^2 \hat{K}_t - \hat{B}_t + q_t g_t \hat{B}_{t+1}.$$

Substituting for $\hat{C}_t$ using the resource constraint, the first-order conditions with respect to $\hat{K}_{t+1}, \hat{B}_{t+1}$, and L_t are

$$u_c(\hat{C}_t, L_t) \left[g_t + \phi \left(g_t \frac{\hat{K}_{t+1}}{\hat{K}_t} - \mu_g \right) g_t \right] = f(\beta, g_t) E_t \left(\frac{\partial V}{\partial \hat{K}_{t+1}} \right), \qquad (1.9)$$

$$u_c(\hat{C}_t, L_t) g_t q_t + f(\beta, g_t) E_t \left(\frac{\partial V}{\partial \hat{B}_{t+1}} \right) = 0, \qquad (1.10)$$

$$u_L(\hat{C}_t, L_t) + u_c(\hat{C}_t, L_t) \frac{\partial \hat{Y}_t}{\partial L_t} = 0. \qquad (1.11)$$

The envelope conditions are given by

$$\frac{\partial V(\hat{K}_t, \hat{B}_t, z_t, g_t)}{\partial \hat{K}_t} = u_c(\hat{C}_t, L_t) \left\{ \frac{\partial \hat{Y}_t}{\partial \hat{K}_t} + (1 - \delta) \right.$$

$$\left. + \phi \left(g_t \frac{\hat{K}_{t+1}}{\hat{K}_t} - \mu_g \right) g_t \frac{\hat{K}_{t+1}}{\hat{K}_t} - \frac{\phi}{2} \left(g_t \frac{\hat{K}_{t+1}}{\hat{K}_t} - \mu_g \right)^2 \right\},$$

$$\frac{\partial V(\hat{K}_t, \hat{B}_t, z_t, g_t)}{\partial \hat{B}_t} = -u_c(\hat{C}_t, L_t).$$

For simplicity, consider only the case with GHH preferences. The stationary competitive equilibrium satisfies the following conditions:

$$(\hat{C}_t - \tau L_t)^{-\sigma} \left(1 + \phi \left(g_t \frac{\hat{K}_{t+1}}{\hat{K}_t} - \mu_g \right) \right)$$

$$= \frac{\beta}{g_t^\sigma} E_t \left\{ (\hat{C}_{t+1} - \tau L_{t+1})^{-\sigma} \left[1 - \delta + \exp(z_{t+1})(1-\alpha) g_{t+1}^\alpha \left(\frac{L_{t+1}}{\hat{K}_{t+1}} \right)^\alpha \right. \right.$$

$$\left. \left. + \phi \left(g_{t+1} \frac{\hat{K}_{t+2}}{\hat{K}_{t+1}} - \mu_g \right) g_{t+1} \frac{\hat{K}_{t+2}}{\hat{K}_{t+1}} - \frac{\phi}{2} \left(g_{t+1} \frac{\hat{K}_{t+2}}{\hat{K}_{t+1}} - \mu_g \right)^2 \right] \right\},$$

(1.12)

$$(\hat{C}_t - \tau L_t^\nu)^{-\sigma} = \frac{\beta(1+r)}{g_t^\sigma} E_t \left[(\hat{C}_{t+1} - \tau L_{t+1}^\nu)^\sigma \right], \qquad (1.13)$$

$$\tau \nu L_t^{\nu-1} = \exp(z_t) \alpha g_t^\alpha \left(\frac{\hat{K}_t}{L_t} \right)^{1-\alpha}, \qquad (1.14)$$

subject to the production function (1.1), the laws of motion for the shocks (1.2)–(1.4), the resource constraint (1.7), and the equation describing the real interest rate (1.8).

The solution for the model is obtained by implementing a log-linear approximation to the equilibrium conditions described above. In the recent applications, a subset of the parameters is set at values determined *a priori*. The remainder of the parameters, including the parameters of the shock processes, are estimated using a generalized method of moments (GMM) approach that we describe in detail in the following chapter.

6.2. DO SHOCKS TO TREND PRODUCTIVITY EXPLAIN BUSINESS CYCLES IN EMERGING MARKET ECONOMIES?

Aguiar and Gopinath [1] consider two versions of their model, an emerging market economy version estimated using quarterly data for Mexico and a developed country version estimated for Canada between 1980 and 2003. The moments that they use for estimation include the standard deviations of log (filtered) income, investment, consumption, net exports-to-GDP, as well as the correlations of the latter three with output. They also consider the mean and standard deviation of (unfiltered) income growth as well as the autocorrelations of (filtered) income and (unfiltered) income growth. This yields 11 moment conditions. The parameters to be estimated are given by $(\mu_g, \sigma_z, \rho_z, \sigma_g, \rho_g, \phi)$. Since the number of parameters is less than the number of moment conditions, there are also overidentifying conditions which can be used to test the model's implications. The most noteworthy finding that emerges from the estimation is that the ratio of shock standard deviations, σ_g/σ_z, is 0.25 or 0.41 for Canada depending on the specification for preferences, and 2.5 or 5.4 for Mexico. This ratio captures the importance of shocks to trend productivity. By contrast, the autocorrelations of transitory shocks are roughly similar, as is the capital adjustment parameter ϕ.

The authors argue that differences in the magnitude of shocks to trend productivity can account for some of the salient features of business cycles in emerging market economies. In particular, they show that a positive transitory shock to productivity reduces consumption in anticipation of lower income in the future. By contrast, a positive shock to trend productivity causes consumption to respond more than output in the expectation that income will be higher in the future. This leads to a large trade deficit which tends to persist for a considerable period of time (16 quarters). Thus, the shock to trend productivity can generate consumption booms that tend to appear side-by-side with current account deficits in emerging market economies. Furthermore, these results can also explain why consumption is more volatile than income in economies where shocks to productivity growth are more important than transitory shocks.

These findings have been challenged by Garcia-Cicco *et al.* [101], who argue that the results of Aguiar and Gopinath [1] are due to their use of a short sample to estimate low-frequency movements in productivity. By contrast, Garcia-Cicco *et al.* [101] use annual data for Argentina over the period 1913–2005. As we described earlier, much of the business cycle literature for developed countries has concentrated on the post-World War II period. Given the evidence that business cycles have moderated during this period, this choice of sample period does not seem out of line. Garcia-Cicco *et al.* [101] argue that a similar finding is not true for an emerging market economy such as Argentina. In particular, they show that output fluctuations in the post-World War II period are as large as those in the pre-World War II period. They consider a model that is very similar to the one in Aguiar and Gopinath [1], and estimate the parameters of the stochastic processes for the permanent and transitory shocks using 16 moment conditions. In particular, they consider the variances and first- and second-order autocorrelations of output growth, consumption growth, investment growth, and the trade balance-to-output ratio; the correlations of output growth with consumption growth, investment growth, and the trade balance-to-output ratio; and the unconditional mean of output growth.

First, unlike Aguiar and Gopinath [1], Garcia-Cicco *et al.* [101] find that the overidentifying restrictions of the model are rejected. Second, in terms of the parameter estimates, the permanent shock is estimated to be more volatile and persistent than the transitory shock. The standard deviations of the shocks and the autoregressive parameter for the permanent shock are estimated precisely. However, this is not the case for the autoregressive coefficient for the transitory shock, which is not significantly different from zero. As we described above, consumption growth will be more volatile than output growth if permanent shocks are more important than transitory shocks, and less volatile than output growth if the opposite is true. They determine this empirically, and find that the consumption-smoothing motive in response to a transitory shock dominates the anticipatory effect of consumption to a permanent productivity shock, and, in contrast to what is observed in the data, consumption growth in the estimated model is calculated to be less volatile than output growth. The authors also find that the trade balance-to-output ratio is estimated to be around four times as volatile as output growth, whereas in the data these quantities are roughly equal. Whereas the first result suggests that the estimated model does not emphasize the role of permanent shocks sufficiently, the second result suggests that it overemphasizes them. Third, investment growth is found to be insufficiently volatile, suggesting in this case that *neither* source of shocks is sufficiently volatile. The authors show that the estimated model also fails to replicate the autocorrelations of output growth and the trade balance-to-output ratio. In particular, the trade balance-to-output ratio displays a near random walk behavior even though the estimated autocorrelation function in the data is downward-sloping. The authors also show that the random walk behavior of the trade balance-to-output ratio remains, regardless of whether shocks to productivity are permanent or transitory. If the shocks are permanent, consumption increases in response to an innovation to output in roughly the same magnitude as output, as households perceive the income increase to be permanent. Hence, the trade balance is unaffected and the trade balance-to-output ratio inherits the behavior of output. By contrast, if the shocks are transitory, the behavior of the trade balance-to-output ratio again follows a near random walk because in this case, with a constant world interest rate, consumption in the model follows a near random walk even though output and investment become stationary variables.

Garcia-Cicco *et al.* [101] conclude that a pure RBC model driven by permanent and/or transitory exogenous shifts in productivity does not provide an adequate explanation of business cycles in emerging markets. In particular, they argue that some of their findings that we described above point to the importance of shocks that are different from productivity shocks. However, they also argue that their results are derived under the joint hypothesis of business cycles driven by productivity shocks and the propagation mechanisms of the standard RBC approach. Hence, their findings cannot be used to disentangle which of these factors is responsible for the failure of the model to replicate the observations.

Chapter 7

Matching the Model to the Data

In the previous chapters, we described some criticisms leveled against the assumptions of the real business cycle (RBC) framework. Amongst the most prominent of these assumptions is the assumption of perfect price flexibility. We also discussed variations of the model that could be used to account for specific correlations in the data. Yet one of the most important aspects of the debate regarding the RBC approach lies in the use of calibration as a way of matching the model to the data. In this chapter, we will study alternative approaches for matching the implications of a theoretical model with the data, and also provide an overview of the estimation versus calibration debate.

The recent business cycle literature has witnessed the use of a variety of techniques regarding the empirics of business cycles. One of the most popular approaches has been based on the dynamic factor model, which seeks to describe the joint cyclical behavior of a key set of time series in terms of a low-dimensional vector of unobservable factors and a set of idiosyncratic shocks. This model was initially proposed by Sargent and Sims [185] for describing cyclical phenomena. In her original contribution, Altug [5] estimated an unobservable index model for a key set of aggregate series based on a modified version of the Kydland and Prescott model [141] using maximum likelihood. Watson [209] extended this approach to derive measures of fit for an underlying economic model. An alternative approach was proposed by Christiano and Eichenbaum [65], who used the generalized method of moments (GMM) approach (see Hansen [113]) to match a selected set of *unconditional* first and second moments implied by their model. Their approach may be viewed as an extension of the standard RBC approach, which assesses the adequacy of the model based on the behavior of the relative variability and co-movement of a small set of moments. Canova [56, 57] discusses alternative approaches for conducting statistical inference in calibrated models. Finally, Bayesian estimation of the so-called dynamic stochastic general equilibrium (DSGE) models provides an alternative to incorporating prior beliefs about various parameters that formalize some of the practices in the calibration approach.

7.1. DYNAMIC FACTOR ANALYSIS

Dynamic factor analysis seeks to describe the joint cyclical behavior of a key set of time series in terms of a low-dimensional vector of unobservable factors and a set of idiosyncratic shocks that are mutually uncorrelated and uncorrelated with the factors. To describe how to formulate unobservable index models, let $\{\tilde{w}_t\}_{t=0}^{\infty}$ denote an n-dimensional mean zero, covariance stationary stochastic process used to describe observations on the (possibly de-trended) values of a set of variables. A k-factor unobservable index model for $\tilde{w}_t$ is given by

$$\tilde{w}_t = \sum_{s=-\infty}^{\infty} \tilde{H}(s)\tilde{f}_{t-s} + \tilde{v}_t, \tag{1.1}$$

where $\{\tilde{H}(s)\}_{s=-\infty}^{\infty}$ is a sequence of $(n \times k)$-dimensional matrices, $\tilde{f}_t$ is a $k \times 1$ vector of common factors, and $\tilde{v}_t$ is an $n \times 1$ vector of idiosyncratic shocks that are mutually uncorrelated and uncorrelated with common factors. More precisely, we require that

$$E(\tilde{f}_t \tilde{v}_{i,t}) = 0 \quad \text{for } i = 1, \ldots, n \tag{1.2}$$

$$E(\tilde{v}_{i,t} \tilde{v}_{j,t}) = 0 \quad \text{for } i \neq j. \tag{1.3}$$

Both the common factors and the idiosyncratic factors may be serially correlated, that is, $E(\tilde{f}_t \tilde{f}_{t-s}) \neq 0$ for $t \neq s$ and $E(\tilde{v}_{i,t} \tilde{v}_{i,t-s}) \neq 0$ for all $i, j, t \neq s$. According to this model, covariation among the elements of $\tilde{w}_t$ can arise because they are functions of the same common factor or because they are functions of different factors which are themselves correlated at different leads and lags.

Under these assumptions, the variances and autocovariances of the observed series $\{\tilde{w}_t\}$ can be decomposed in terms of the variances and autocovariances of a low-dimensional set of unobserved common factors and the idiosyncratic shocks. Let

$$R_w(r) = E(\tilde{w}_t(\tilde{w}_{t+r})'), \quad r = \ldots, -1, 0, 1, \ldots$$

be the autocovariance function of $\{\tilde{w}_t\}$. Under the assumptions underlying (1.1),

$$R_w(r) = E\left[\left(\sum_{s=-\infty}^{\infty} \tilde{H}(s)\tilde{f}_{t-s} + \tilde{v}_t\right)\left(\sum_{v=-\infty}^{\infty} \tilde{H}(v)\tilde{f}_{t+r-v} + \tilde{v}_{t+r}\right)'\right]$$

$$= E\left[\left(\cdots + \tilde{H}(-1)\tilde{f}_{t+1} + \tilde{H}(0)\tilde{f}_t + \tilde{H}(1)\tilde{f}_{t-1} + \cdots + \tilde{v}_t\right)\right.$$

$$\left. \times \left(\cdots + \tilde{H}(-1)\tilde{f}_{t+r+1} + \tilde{H}(0)\tilde{f}_{t+r} + \tilde{H}(1)\tilde{f}_{t+r-1} + \cdots + \tilde{v}_{t+r}\right)'\right]$$

$$= \sum_{s=-\infty}^{\infty} \tilde{H}(s) \sum_{v=-\infty}^{\infty} E(\tilde{f}_{t-s}\tilde{f}_{t+r-v})\tilde{H}(v) + E(\tilde{v}_t\tilde{v}_{t+r})$$

$$= \sum_{s=-\infty}^{\infty} \tilde{H}(s) \sum_{v=-\infty}^{\infty} R_f(r+s-v)\tilde{H}(v)' + R_v(r).$$

An alternative representation of the autocovariance function is provided by the spectral density function

$$S_w(\omega) = \sum_{r=\infty}^{\infty} R_w(r)e^{-ir\omega}, \quad |\omega| \le \pi.^{[1]} \tag{1.4}$$

Assuming that $S_w(\omega)$ is non-singular at each frequency ω, notice that off-diagonal elements of $S_w(\omega)$ are, in general, complex numbers. However, since $R_{x_l x_h}(r) = R_{x_l x_h}(-r)$, the diagonal elements of $S_w(\omega)$ are real. Substituting for $R_w(r)$ into (1.4) yields

$$S_w(\omega) = \sum_{r=\infty}^{\infty} \sum_{s=-\infty}^{\infty} \tilde{H}(s) \sum_{v=-\infty}^{\infty} R_f(r+s-v)\tilde{H}(v)' \exp(-i\omega r)$$

$$+ \sum_{r=\infty}^{\infty} S_v(r) \exp(-i\omega r)$$

---

[1] This function is well-defined as long as $\sum_{r=-\infty}^{\infty} R_{x_l x_h}^2(r) < \infty$ for each $l, h = 1, \ldots, n$.

$$= \sum_{s=-\infty}^{\infty} \tilde{H}(s) \exp(-i\omega s) \sum_{u=-\infty}^{\infty} R_w(u) \exp(-i\omega u)$$

$$\times \sum_{z=-\infty}^{\infty} \tilde{H}(z)' \exp(-i\omega z) + S_v(\omega)$$

$$= \tilde{H}(\omega) S_w(\omega) \tilde{H}(\omega)' + S_v(\omega),$$

where $\tilde{H}(\omega)$ denotes the Fourier transform of $\tilde{H}(s)$. Hence, the dynamic factor model provides decomposition at each frequency that is analogous to the decomposition of variance in the conventional factor model. The dynamic factor model can be estimated and its restrictions tested across alternative frequencies using a frequency domain approach to time series analysis. The unrestricted version of the dynamic factor model does not place restrictions on the matrices $\tilde{H}(s)$, which describe how the common factors affect the behavior of the elements of $\tilde{w}_t$ at all leads and lags. Also, it is not possible to identify the common factors with different types of shocks to the economy.

The use of the dynamic factor model in business cycle analysis dates back to the work of Sargent and Sims [185]. As these authors observe, dynamic factor analysis may be linked to the notion of a "reference cycle" underlying the methodology of Burns and Mitchell [50] and the empirical business cycle literature they conducted at the National Bureau of Economic Research. Another well-known application of this approach is due to Altug [5], who derives an unobservable index model for a key set of aggregate series by augmenting the approximate linear decision rules for a modified version of the Kydland and Prescott [141] model with i.i.d. error terms. Sargent [184] also employs the device of augmenting a singular model with additional idiosyncratic shocks. He discusses a classical measurement error case, as in Altug [5], as well as a case with orthogonal prediction errors. Altug also uses this representation to estimate the model using maximum likelihood (ML) estimation in the frequency domain. The restricted factor model makes use of the cross-equation restrictions across the linear decision rules implied by the original model. The common factor is identified as the innovation to the technology shock, and the idiosyncratic shocks are interpreted as i.i.d. measurement errors or idiosyncratic components not captured by the underlying RBC model. Unlike the unrestricted factor model which can be estimated frequency by frequency, this model must be estimated jointly across all frequencies because the underlying economic model constrains the dynamic behavior of the different series as well as specifies the nature of the unobserved factor.[2] Altug [5] initially estimates an unrestricted dynamic factor model for the level of per capita hours and the differences in per capita values of durable goods consumption, investment in equipment, investment in structures, and aggregate output. She finds that the hypothesis of a single unobservable factor cannot be rejected at conventional significance levels for describing the joint time series behavior of the variables. However, when the restrictions of the underlying model are imposed, the model cannot explain the cyclical variation of the observed variables.

7.1.1. *Measures of Fit for Calibrated Models*

Watson [209] extended the approach in Altug [5] and Sargent [184] to derive measures of fit for an underlying economic model. Unlike the approach adopted by Altug and Sargent, Watson's analysis does not depend on assuming that the unobserved factors and the idiosyncratic shocks are uncorrelated. Instead, his approach involves choosing the correlation properties of the error process between the actual data and the underlying model such that its variance is as small as possible. Also, the joint process for the data and the error is introduced to motivate goodness-of-fit measures, not to describe a statistical model that can be used to conduct statistical tests.

To describe Watson's approach, let x_t denote an $n \times 1$ vector of covariance stationary random variables. Define the autocovariance generating function (ACGF) for x_t by

$$A_x(z) = \sum_{r=-\infty}^{\infty} E(x_t x_{t-r}) z^r.$$

Here, $\{x_t\}_{t=0}^{\infty}$ denotes the stochastic process generated by some underlying model, and A_x summarizes the unconditional second-moment properties of this model. In the data, the vector of variables y_t corresponds to the empirical counterpart of x_t. The ACGF for y_t is similarly denoted $A_y(z)$. The question at hand is whether the data generated by the model are able to reproduce the behavior of the observed series. For this purpose, define the $n \times 1$ vector of

---

[2]For further discussion of maximum likelihood estimation in the frequency domain, see Hansen and Sargent [114].

errors u_t that are required to reconcile the ACGF implied by the model with that of the data.[3]

To continue, define u_t by the relation

$$u_t = y_t - x_t, \tag{1.5}$$

which implies that the ACGF for u_t can be expressed as

$$A_u(z) = A_y(z) + A_x(z) - A_{xy}(z) + A_{yx}(z), \tag{1.6}$$

where $A_{xy}(z)$ is the joint ACGF for x_t and y_t. To calculate $A_u(z)$, notice that $A_y(z)$ can be determined from the data, and $A_x(z)$ from the model. However, since $A_{xy}(z)$ is unknown, some additional assumptions are needed to operationalize this approach. In the standard dynamic factor model, the assumption regarding $A_{xy}(z)$ is that it is zero, $A_{xy}(z) = 0$. This implies a version of a classical errors-in-variables approach.[4] However, in Watson's framework, the error term u_t is the approximation error in describing the observed data with the underlying economic model. Hence, the assumption of pure measurement error which is uncorrelated with the true variable is not appropriate. Nevertheless, a lower bound may be deduced for the variance of u_t without imposing any restrictions on $A_{xy}(z)$. This bound is calculated by choosing $A_{xy}(z)$ to minimize the variance of u_t subject to the constraint that the implied joint ACGF for x_t and y_t is positive definite.

To illustrate this approach, let us consider two cases.[5] In the first case, x_t, y_t, and u_t are assumed to be serially uncorrelated scalar random variables. The problem is to choose σ_{xy} to minimize the variance of u_t subject to the constraint that the covariance matrix of x_t and y_t remains positive definite, or $|\sigma_{xy}| \leq \sigma_x \sigma_y$:

$$\min_{\sigma_{xy}} \sigma_u^2 = \sigma_y^2 + \sigma_x^2 - 2\sigma_{xy} \text{ s.t. } |\sigma_{xy}| \leq \sigma_x \sigma_y. \tag{1.7}$$

---

[3] In a standard goodness-of-fit approach, it is the size of the sampling error that is used to judge whether a given model fits that data. In this case, let $A_y(z)$ denote the population autocovariance function and $\hat{A}_y(z)$ denote its estimated counterpart. Then, the difference between $A_y(z)$ and $\hat{A}_y(z)$ is ascribed to sampling error, and the size of the sampling error can be determined from the data-generating process for y_t. If, in addition, $A_y(z) = A_x(z)$, then the sampling error in estimating $A_y(z)$ from actual data can also be used to determine how different $A_y(z)$ is from $A_x(z)$.

[4] This is similar to the interpretation provided by Altug [5].

[5] We omit the third case that Watson considers because it requires results for the Cramer representation of stationary time series.

It is easy to see that the solution for this problem is to set $\sigma_{xy} = \sigma_x \sigma_y$. As a consequence, $\sigma_u^2 = (\sigma_y - \sigma_x)^2$ at the minimum. Furthermore, x_t and y_t are perfectly correlated so that

$$x_t = \gamma y_t, \qquad (1.8)$$

where $\gamma = \sigma_x / \sigma_y$.

Now suppose that x_t and y_t are serially uncorrelated random vectors with covariance matrices Σ_x and Σ_y. The covariance matrix of u_t is given by $\Sigma_u = \Sigma_y + \Sigma_x - \Sigma_{xy} + \Sigma_{yx}$. In this case, we cannot minimize the variance of u_t directly. Instead, we consider a transformation that allows us to determine the size of u_t. One convenient transformation is the trace of Σ_u, $tr(\Sigma_u) = \sum_{i=1}^{n} \Sigma_{ij,u}$, where $\Sigma_{ij,u}$ denotes the i,j element of Σ. An alternative approach is to minimize the weighted sum of the variances as $tr(W\Sigma_u)$, where W is an $n \times n$ matrix. The problem in this case is to choose Σ_{xy} to minimize $tr(W\Sigma_u)$ subject to the constraint that the covariance matrix of (x_t', y_t') is positive semi-definite. Watson [209] provides a solution for the case in which Σ_x has rank $k \leq n$ so that the number of variables is typically less than the number of shocks. Proposition 1 in Watson [209] demonstrates that the unique matrix Σ_{xy}, which minimizes the weighted sum of the variances of the elements of u_t subject to the constraint that this matrix is positive semidefinite, is given by

$$\Sigma_{xy} = C_x V U C_y'. \qquad (1.9)$$

In this expression, C_x is the $n \times k$ matrix square root of Σ_x as $\Sigma_x = C_x C_x'$ and C_y is the $n \times n$ matrix square root of Σ_y. The matrices U and V are defined from the singular value decomposition USV' of $C_y' W C_x$ such that U is a $n \times k$ orthogonal matrix (with $U'U = I_k$), V is a $k \times k$ orthonormal matrix (with $VV' = I_k$), and S is a $k \times k$ diagonal matrix. An implication of this result is that, as in the scalar case, the joint covariance matrix of (x_t', y_t') is singular. As a consequence, x_t can be represented as

$$x_t = \Gamma y_t, \qquad (1.10)$$

where $\Gamma = C_x U V C_y^{-1}$. For $k = 1$, this result corresponds to the one in the scalar case, given the properties of the U and V matrices.

Watson [209] uses this methodology to generate goodness-of-fit measures for a standard RBC model with a stochastic trend in technology. Specifically, he considers the model in King, Plosser, and Rebelo [131, 132]. He log-linearizes the first-order conditions to obtain the solution for log-differences of output, consumption, investment, and the number of hours worked. His approach allows for a decomposition by frequency of the variance in each observed series, the variance explained by the model, and the error in reconciling the model with the data.[6] He finds that the biggest differences between the spectra for output, consumption, and investment occur at frequencies corresponding to the business cycle periodicities of 6–32 quarters. The model also implies that the number of hours worked is stationary whereas there is considerable power at the low frequencies for this series in the data, suggesting that the stochastic trend properties of the model do not hold in the data. Watson's analysis shows that focusing only on a small subset of moments implied by the model can be misleading because the RBC model is unable to reproduce the typical spectral shape of economic time series.

7.1.2. *Other Applications*

Forni and Reichlin [93] use the dynamic factor model to describe business cycle dynamics for large cross-sections. Based on a law of large numbers argument, they show that the number of common factors can be determined using the method of principal components, the economy-wide shocks can be identified using structural vector autoregression (SVAR) techniques, and the unobserved factor model can be estimated by using equation-by-equation ordinary least squares (OLS). They examine the behavior of four-digit industrial output and productivity for the US economy for the period 1958–1986 and find evidence in favor of at least two economy-wide shocks, both having a long-run effect on sectoral output. However, their results also indicate that sector-specific shocks are needed to explain the variance of the series.

Giannone, Reichlin, and Sala [103] show how more general classes of equilibrium business cycle models can be cast in terms of the dynamic factor representation. They also describe how to derive impulse response functions for time series models which have reduced rank, that is, models for which the number of exogenous shocks is less than the number of series.

---

[6]A comparison of the spectra implied by the model and those generated by actual data also figured in early versions of Altug [5]; see also Altug [4].

7.2. GMM ESTIMATION APPROACHES

Other papers have employed nonlinear estimation and inference techniques to match equilibrium business models with the data. Christiano and Eichenbaum [65] consider the hours-productivity puzzle and use the generalized method of moments (GMM) approach (see Hansen [113]) to match a selected set of *unconditional* first and second moments implied by their model. Their approach may be viewed as an extension of the standard RBC approach, which assesses the adequacy of the model based on the behavior of the relative variability and co-movement of a small set of time series.

Christiano and Eichenbaum [65] derive a solution for the social planner's problem by implementing a quadratic approximation to the original nonlinear problem around the deterministic steady states. Since there is a stochastic trend in this economy arising from the nature of the technology shock process, the deterministic steady states are derived for the transformed variables. Their estimation strategy is based on a subset of the first and second moments implied by their model. To describe how their approach is implemented, let Ψ_1 denote a vector of parameters determining preferences, technology, and the exogenous stochastic processes. Some of the parameters included in Ψ_1 may be the depreciation rate of capital, δ, and the share of capital in the neoclassical production function, θ. More generally, $\Psi_1 = (\delta, \theta, \gamma, \rho, \bar{g}, \sigma_\mu, \lambda, \sigma_\lambda)'$. As in the standard RBC approach, the parameters in Ψ_1 are estimated using simple first-moment restrictions implied by the model. For example, the depreciation rate δ is set to reproduce the average depreciation on capital as

$$E\left\{\delta - \left[1 - \frac{i_t}{k_t} - \frac{k_{t+1}}{k_t}\right]\right\} = 0,$$

given data on gross investment i_t and the capital stock k_{t+1}. Likewise, the share of capital satisfies the Euler equation

$$E\left\{\beta^{-1}\left[\theta\left(\frac{y_{t+1}}{k_{t+1}}\right) + 1 - \delta\right]\frac{c_t}{c_{t+1}}\right\} = 0.$$

Proceeding in this way, the elements of Ψ_1 satisfy the unconditional moment restrictions

$$E\left[H_{1t}(\Psi_1)\right] = 0. \tag{2.11}$$

The elements of Ψ_2 consist of the standard RBC second-moment restrictions as

$$E\left[y_t^2(\sigma_x/\sigma_y)^2 - x_t^2\right] = 0, \quad x = c_t, i_t, g_t, \quad (2.12)$$

$$E\left[n_t^2 - \sigma_n^2\right] = 0, \quad (2.13)$$

$$E\left\{(y/n)_t^2 \left(\sigma_n/\sigma_{y/n}\right)^2 - n_t^2\right\} = 0, \quad (2.14)$$

$$E\left\{\left[\sigma_n^2/(\sigma_n/\sigma_{y/n})\right] corr(y/n, n) - (y/n)_t n_t\right\} = 0, \quad (2.15)$$

where c_t denotes private consumption; i_t, private investment; g_t, public consumption; n_t, labor hours; and $(y/n)_t$, the average productivity of labor. The unconditional second moments are obtained through simulating the model's solution based on the linear decision rules obtained from the approximate social planner's problem. The restrictions of the model can be summarized as

$$E\left[H_{2t}(\Psi_2)\right] = 0. \quad (2.16)$$

Christiano and Eichenbaum [65] are interested in testing restrictions for the correlation between hours and productivity, $corr(y/n, n)$, and the relative variability of hours versus average productivity, $\sigma_n/\sigma_{y/n}$. To do this, they use a Wald-type test based on the orthogonality conditions implied by the relevant unconditional moments. For any parameter vector Ψ_1, let

$$f(\Psi_1) = [f_1(\Psi_1), f_2(\Psi_1)]' \quad (2.17)$$

represent the model's restrictions for $corr(y/n, n)$ and $\sigma_n/\sigma_{y/n}$. Define $\Psi = [\Psi_1, \Psi_2]'$ as the $k \times 1$ vector containing the true values of the parameters and second moments for the model. Also, let A be a $2 \times k$ matrix of zeros and ones such that

$$A\Psi = [corr(y/n, n), \sigma_n/\sigma_{y/n}]' \quad (2.18)$$

and

$$F(\Psi) = f(\Psi_1) - A\Psi. \quad (2.19)$$

Under the null hypothesis that the model is correctly specified,

$$F(\Psi) = 0. \quad (2.20)$$

In practice, there is sampling error in estimating Ψ from a finite data set containing T observations. Letting $\hat{\Psi}_T$ denote the estimated value of Ψ, the test statistic for the second-moment restrictions is based on the distribution of $F(\hat{\Psi}_T)$ under the null hypothesis. Using this distribution, the authors show that the statistic

$$J = F(\hat{\Psi}_T)' Var[F(\hat{\Psi}_T)]^{-1} F(\hat{\Psi}_T) \tag{2.21}$$

is asymptotically distributed as a χ^2 random variable with two degrees of freedom.

Using data on private consumption, government expenditures, investment, aggregate hours, and average productivity, Christiano and Eichenbaum [65] estimate the parameters of the model using GMM and examine the various unconditional second moments implied by the model. As we described earlier, the GMM approach has been used in other recent applications. For example, Aguiar and Gopinath [1] and Garcia-Cicco, Pancrazi, and Uribe [101] employ this approach in their analysis of business cycles in emerging markets.

7.3. THE CALIBRATION VERSUS ESTIMATION DEBATE

The crux of the recent business cycle debate centers on how a given theoretical model should be matched with the data. Kydland and Prescott [141] initiated this debate in the modern business cycle literature. Since then, there have been ongoing discussions on both sides of the issue.[7] In this section, we will deal with a variety of criticisms aimed directly at the calibration approach and some suggested alternatives to it.

In a highly suggestive analysis, Eichenbaum [82] asked whether RBC analysis, in fact, constituted "wisdom or whimsy". He took issue with the calibration approach by showing that the model's implications for the variance of output relative to its value in the data are heavily dependent on assumed values for the underlying parameters for the technology process. In his words:

> Indeed, once we quantify the uncertainty in model predictions arising from uncertainty about model parameter values, calibrated or otherwise, our view of what the data is [*sic*] telling us is affected in a first-order way. Even if

---

[7] See Kydland and Prescott [142, 143] for a further discussion and defense of their approach.

we do not perturb the standard theory and even if we implement existing formulations of that theory on the standard postwar sample period and even if we use the stationary inducing transformation of the data that has become standard in RBC studies — even then the strong conclusions which mark this literature are unwarranted. What the data are actually telling us is that, while technology shocks almost certainly play some role in generating the business cycle, there is simply an enormous amount of uncertainty of just what percent of aggregate fluctuations they actually do account for. The answer could be 70% as Kydland and Prescott [142] claim, but the data contain almost no evidence against either the view that the answer is really 5% or that the answer is really 200%.

Eichenbaum [82] also presented evidence to show that the performance of the standard model as well as modifications that allow for labor hoarding, for example, deteriorate considerably when a break in the sample is allowed for. Such a break accounts for the slowdown in productivity growth in the US that occurred in the late 1960s.

7.3.1. *The Dynamics of Output*

Cogley and Nason [70] examine the dynamics of output as a way of determining the efficacy of the RBC model in describing the data. As part of their diagnostics, they consider the autocorrelation function for output, its power spectrum, and impulse response functions in response to shocks. Since the single technology shock model is singular, they use the two-shock version of the RBC model proposed by Christiano and Eichenbaum [65], which includes shocks to productivity and government consumption as well as the indivisible labor feature of Hansen [112] and Rogerson [179]. They assume that the technology shocks are difference-stationary, whereas government shocks evolve as a persistent AR(1) process. To estimate impulse response functions from the data, the authors use the SVAR technique developed by Blanchard and Quah [43]. They consider a two-variable VAR with output and hours worked (or consumption), and identify the technology shock under the assumption that it has a permanent effect on output. They compare the autocorrelation function and the impulse response function in the data with those generated by the model using generalized Q statistics. The autocorrelation function from the model is generated by simulating the model 1000 times. The striking results in Cogley and Nason [70] show that the autocorrelation function for output implied by the model is nearly flat, as is the power spectrum.[8] By contrast, the autocorrelations of output at lags 1 and 2 are significant and positive, and the spectrum for output displays significant power at the business cycle frequencies of 2.33–7 years per cycle. The test statistic also shows that the implications of the model are rejected at significance levels of 1% or less. In terms of the impulse response functions, the model has some success in matching the estimated response functions in the data for the permanent component of GDP, but it is unable to match the impulse response function for the transitory component. In particular, the data display a hump-shaped response to transitory shocks whereas the model implies a much smaller monotonic decay. Cogley and Nason [70] also argue that the model displays weak propagation mechanisms which arise from intertemporal substitution, capital accumulation, and adjustment costs.

7.3.2. *Calibration as Estimation*

Canova [56, 57] proposes an alternative approach for providing statistical inference in calibrated models. His approach involves constructing prior distributions for the parameters used in calibrated models based on existing estimates in the literature or other *a priori* information available to the researcher. To describe his approach, let $\bar{X}_t$ denote a vector stochastic process with a known distribution that describes the evolution of a set of observed variables, say, GDP, investment, and interest rates. Also, let $X_t = f(Z_t, \beta)$ denote the process for these variables generated by a specific economic theory or model as a function of exogenous and predetermined variables Z_t and the parameters β. Let $G(X_t|f, \beta)$ denote the density of the vector X_t, conditional on the function f and the parameters β; let $\pi(\beta|I, f)$ denote the density for the parameters β, conditional on the information set available to the researcher I and the function f; and let $H(X_t, \beta|f, I)$ denote the joint density for the data and the parameters. Denote the predictive density $p(X_t|I, f) = \int H(X_t, \beta|I, f)d\beta$. Define expectations of the functions of the simulated data

---

[8]These results are, in some sense, complementary to those regarding the role of filtering on the cyclical properties generated from a standard RBC model. See Cogley and Nason [69].

(denoted by $\mu(X_t)$) under the predictive distribution $p(X_t|I,f)$ by

$$E(\mu(X_t)|f,I) = \int \mu(X_t)p(X_t|I,f)dX_t$$

$$= \int \int H(X_t,\beta|I,f)d\beta dX_t. \qquad (3.22)$$

This approach allows for a probability statement regarding the behavior of various moments implied by the model. More precisely, suppose that we are interested in evaluating $Pr(v(X_t) \in D)$, where $v(X_t)$ is some moment of interest and D is a bounded set. Then, define $\mu(X_t) = 1$ if $v(X_t) \in D$ and zero otherwise. Notice also that the function f is typically unknown and must be obtained using some approximation method. Canova [56] describes how to account for such an approximation error when computing the moments of the simulated data. While the densities H and p are unknown, the model can be simulated repeatedly for different values of β and Z_t to compute sample paths for X_t. In general, the approach that Canova advocates for conducting statistical inference in calibrated models is as follows:

- Select a density $\pi(\beta|I,f)$ for the unknown parameters, given the information I available to the researcher and a density $k(Z_t)$ for the exogenous processes.
- Draw vectors β from $\pi(\beta|I,f)$ and z_t from $k(Z_t)$.
- For each drawing of β and z_t, generate $\{x_t\}_{t=1}^T$ and compute $\mu(x_t)$ using the model $x_t = f(z_t,\beta)$ or its approximation.
- Repeat the above two steps N times.
- Construct the frequency distribution of $\mu(x_t)$ and other statistics of interest that can be used to evaluate the performance of the model.

One of the key aspects of Canova's approach is the selection of a density π that summarizes information about existing parameter estimates in an efficient manner. This information may be derived from alternative data sets, model specifications, or estimation techniques. For example, one could count estimates of elements of β obtained from alternative studies and smooth the resulting histogram to obtain the density $\pi(\beta|I,f)$. If such information is hard to obtain, then one can use a uniform distribution. The calibration approach involves putting a point mass on a particular value of β. Simulation exercises conducted after a subset of the parameters has been estimated (using GMM, for example) involve putting a point mass on β^* estimated according to a particular method, say, GMM. One can argue that the approach described above is a global sensitivity exercise that also allows for an evaluation of the model based on the probabilities attached to events that the researcher is interested in.

7.3.3. *Nonlinearity in Macroeconomic Time Series*

Another criticism of the RBC model literature is that it has typically been concerned with examining the first- and second-moment properties of aggregate economic variables for the purpose of matching a model to the data. Yet there is a new literature that shows that macroeconomic time series may exhibit marked nonlinear behavior. Such nonlinearities may take the form of conditional heteroscedasticity such as ARCH or GARCH effects. Alternatively, there may exist asymmetries in various economic variables.

Neftci [166] was among the first to demonstrate that unemployment fluctuations were asymmetrical along the business cycle. Brock and Sayers [47] tested real macroeconomic variables displayed by deterministic chaotic dynamics; and while they could not find evidence of chaotic behavior, they nevertheless showed that postwar employment, unemployment, and industrial production could be described as nonlinear stochastic processes. Ashley and Patterson [22] developed a test to test for deviation from linear stochastic processes, either in the form of nonlinear stochastic dynamics or deterministic chaos. They found strong evidence of nonlinearity in industrial production, and argued that any reasonable macroeconomic model should display some form of nonlinear dynamics (see Potter [172] for a review). In our discussion in Chapter 3, we discussed the role of alternative factors that could give rise to endogenous changes in productivity such as labor hoarding, variable capacity utilization, increasing returns, and time-varying markups. In a novel analysis, Altug, Ashley, and Patterson [9] examine the implied behavior of output, the factor inputs, and the underlying productivity shocks using a simple production function framework. Specifically, they note that observed measures of output and factor inputs such as the capital stock and hours worked display marked nonlinear behavior. Using an array of diagnostic tests, they do not find evidence of nonlinearity in the Solow residuals measured after allowing for increasing returns to scale, markups, or variable capacity utilization. They conclude that the nonlinearity must lie in the transmission mechanism.

Valderrama [207] examines the statistical behavior of national income and product account aggregates for the US and a set of OECD countries including France, Italy, Japan, Mexico, and the UK; and shows that nonlinearities such as skewness, kurtosis, and conditional heteroscedasticity are common for many of these aggregates. He argues that standard general equilibrium models are able to replicate the first- and second-moment properties of such variables, but they are unable to reproduce nonlinearities in these time series. He poses this as a "canonical" challenge to the RBC approach. Valderrama [207] considers a simple Brock–Mirman-type growth model with GHH preferences (see Greenwood, Hercowitz, and Huffman [105]) and adjustment costs in investment. A value iteration approach is used as the solution procedure. This ensures that the nonlinearities in the underlying model are not eliminated through a linearization procedure. The approach to matching the model to the data is through the efficient method of moments (EMM) developed by Gallant and Tauchen [99], which is a two-step procedure. In the first step, a seminonparametric (SNP) model is estimated to characterize the statistical properties of the data. The statistical models are flexible enough to allow for increasing time dependence in the mean of the process (captured through a VAR), for conditional heteroscedasticity (ARCH, GARCH), and for nonnormal disturbances. In the second step, the economic model is simulated for a given set of parameters. A comparison is made between the statistical parameter estimates in the SNP step and the statistical parameters obtained using the simulated data and the same statistical model. Then, the candidate parameters of the simulated model are adjusted until the simulations of the economic model have statistical properties similar to those of the data. The objective function is distributed as a X^2 statistic, as in the GMM approach.

Valderrama [207] selects three statistical models to describe the properties of the data. The SNP approach nests standard VARs. However, it also allows for periods of high volatility followed by low volatility (conditional heteroscedasticity), asymmetric business cycles (i.e., skewness), and excess volatility (i.e., excess kurtosis). The SNP approach uses a standard VAR to model the conditional mean and an ARCH-GARCH structure to model the conditional variance, and it allows for a non-Gaussian error term. The last feature is achieved by taking a transformation of the normal density using Hermite polynomials (see Gallant and Tauchen [100]). The first model selected by the SNP is a VAR(3) with conditional heteroscedasticity and a Hermite polynomial of degree 4. Two other models are selected for the purpose of describing the data. The first of these is a linear VAR(3) so that the statistical procedure is similar to the RBC approach of matching the impulse responses from a standard VAR with those generated from the underlying economic model. The second model is a VAR(3) with ARCH(1) errors, which allows for nonlinearity in terms of the ARCH effects but continues to assume that the errors are Gaussian. The parameters of the underlying economic model are chosen based on standard calibration exercises and also to match the three statistical models using a simulated method of moments approach.

Valderrama [207] finds that the biggest difference among the three statistical models is in terms of the adjustment cost parameter, ϕ. When the statistical model is forced to be a linear VAR(3), this parameter is estimated to be around 10; whereas in the other two models, its estimates are around 3. The intuition for this result stems from the fact that a high adjustment cost parameter helps to smooth the implied behavior of investment and to reduce conditional volatility or kurtosis in the investment series. By contrast, the other two statistical models allow for these features and hence do not require such a high adjustment cost parameter. The linear VAR(3) model also implies a much lower volatility for the consumption and investment series than the other two models. Valderrama finds that the RBC model is not successful at generating the conditional variance of investment; it can capture the nonlinearity in investment, but not the nonlinearity in consumption. Combined with the findings of Altug *et al.* [9] who show that the nonlinearities in the observed series must lie in the propagation mechanism, these results suggest that such features as financial frictions or irreversibility in investment are required to match the nonlinearities of consumption and investment.

Surprisingly, Valderrama [207] finds that the irreversibility constraint does not bind during the solution of the model, implying that the irreversibility feature is not important for matching the model to the data. This is similar to some earlier results in the literature. Veracierto [208] and Thomas [205] compare model economies with irreversible investment (in the case of Veracierto) or lumpy investment (in the case of Thomas) with the actual economy and with a baseline model of flexible investment, and arrive at results that indicate little or no significant impact of irreversibility or lumpiness on aggregate investment dynamics. Veracierto [208] argues that the reason why irreversibility has an impact on aggregate investment in various multi-sector growth models considered in the literature (see, for example, Coleman [73] or Ramey and Shapiro [174]) is due to their assumption of unrealistically large sectoral shocks. Similarly, the reason why aggregate investment displays lower variability in the presence of irreversibility when firms are subject to idiosyncratic shocks, as in Bertola and Caballero [42], is due to their assumption of a very large variance for these idiosyncratic shocks. Veracierto [208] argues that when the size of sectoral shocks is consistent with that observed in the data, the aggregate impact of irreversible investment disappears in a general equilibrium framework. More generally, both Veracierto and Thomas find that irreversibility or lumpiness at the plant level does not affect aggregate investment significantly once general equilibrium effects such as endogenous price adjustments are taken into account. However, this is a puzzling finding. As Caballero [53] emphasizes: "An important point to note is that since only aggregate data were used, these microeconomic nonlinearities must matter at the aggregate level, for otherwise they would not be identified."

Yet, our analysis of the simple RBC model with flexible prices and wages suggests that it cannot successfully match many features of the data. Given the importance of nonlinearity in macroeconomic time series documented in a number of studies, we suggest that the reason why irreversibility may not matter in a model with *flexible* prices is that the introduction of imperfect competition with optimal price-setting behavior on the part of firms or, alternatively, changing the way in which the labor market is modeled and introducing wage contracts in the RBC framework may lead to more pronounced quantity adjustments. Both Veracierto [208] and Thomas [205] assume that labor is perfectly mobile across plants. This latter feature may compensate for the rigidity faced by plants given that capital and labor are substitutable according to the Cobb–Douglas specification of technology, and may be responsible for softening the impact of the inflexibility faced by plants in terms of their capital adjustments. Moreover, as Valderrama [207] states, irreversibility may play a more important role when financial constraints at the plant level and the household level are taken into account. At the same time, one may consider the impact of another type of aggregate shock, namely, monetary shocks. Thus, for example, financial accelerator models of investment find that financially constrained firms' investment responds three times as strongly to a monetary expansion than that of firms which are not constrained (see Bernanke, Gertler, and Gilchrist [41]). These arguments suggest that nonlinearities are another area where the assumptions of the simple RBC model fail to hold, and a potential direction for improving the model's fit.

7.3.4. *The Debate Reconsidered*

King [128] discusses the arguments on different sides of the debate under the heading "Quantitative Theory and Econometrics". King claims to be on the quantitative theory side of the debate, and argues against the estimation and comparison of a "heavily restricted linear time series model (for example, an RBC model with some or all of its parameters estimated) to an unrestricted time series model. For some time, the outcome of this procedure will be known in advance of the test: the probability that the model is true is zero for stochastically singular models and nearly zero for all other models of interest." Returning to the inception of the estimation versus calibration debate, we note that Altug's [4] results did not lead to support for the model. Many have argued that this was to be expected (see Hartley, Hoover, and Salyer [116], p. 17). Yet, Watson's [209] insights were partly due to Altug's initial analysis based on the spectra implied by the model and those in the data.[9] In the absence of the initial frequency-domain estimation based on the factor representation, it is unlikely that RBC models would be subjected to the types of diagnostic tests proposed by Watson [209]. The factor representation underlying Altug's analysis has also been resuscitated by Giannone *et al.* [103] in a VAR framework.

One can also examine the claim that a less restrictive approach to estimation and model evaluation following the approach in Christiano and Eichenbaum [65], for example, may be preferable. King [128] advocates such an approach as an alternative to calibration that does not face the problems of "testing highly restrictive linear models". Yet, one could argue that the GMM approach in Christiano and Eichenbaum [65] involves choosing a subset of moments of an equally restrictive nonlinear model. If the simple model is counterfactual, in what sense does adding another simple feature to such a contrived model "resolve" a very specific empirical puzzle? Adding another shock may "loosen" the behavior of the model, but in what sense does this make the model a better interpretation of reality? King also discusses the shortcomings of this approach, highlighting problems in finding appropriate

---

[9]See Altug [4].

instruments and in the appropriate selection of moment conditions for model evaluation. Gregory and Smith [108] have also argued that the small-sample properties of the estimators obtained with the approach advocated by Christiano and Eichenbaum [65] may be far from reasonable if the calibrated parameters do not consistently estimate the true values.

These arguments show that there is no clear-cut dichotomy between these approaches. The estimation and testing of a highly restrictive linear or linearized model may yield many insights regarding the failure of a model as much as examining the performance of a model based on a small subset of moments. These developments show that the contribution of the more formal econometric techniques need not be dismissed as cursorily as is sometimes the case. Conversely, one could argue that the approach in Christiano and Eichenbaum [65] is *too* restrictive. As Geweke [102] notes, examining a small set of moments does not necessarily lead to a less restrictive approach because the moments under consideration typically incorporate all the implications of the underlying theoretical model. In this sense, examining a broader set of moments may make more sense because this yields more information about the underlying behavior of the model. One interpretation of quantitative theorizing is that it helps researchers understand the workings of highly non-linear dynamic stochastic models and gain some intuition about different model features. This interpretation precludes the notion that quantitative theorizing can take the place of formal econometric methods. It is also worth noting that many of the implications of the standard RBC model have not withstood the scrutiny conducted under a variety of approaches. The simple propagation mechanisms inherent in the model have been deemed incapable of reproducing business cycle dynamics of key variables such as output, and the New Keynesian challenge has shown that the model fails in generating the observed negative response of hours to productivity improvements. Another criticism of the RBC approach is that it fails to capture nonlinearities in key macroeconomic time series.

Perhaps initially the RBC theorists were concerned that the estimation versus calibration debate would discredit the use of well-specified dynamic general equilibrium models for the purpose of capturing the quantitative behavior of economic variables. In fact, far from this occurring, the estimation versus calibration debate has led to a panoply of research that has extended the use of these models in a variety of directions. The initial criticisms of the RBC approach have led to a wide set of extensions of the original RBC approach. As we discuss in the next chapter, the original RBC approach has even instigated a new generation of Keynesian models that offer features such as credit accelerators, sunspot equilibria, and animal spirits. Another extension of the original approach has been the development of applications that are useful for policy analysis, a topic to which we turn next.

7.4. DSGE MODELING

Another offshoot of the original RBC debate is the development of dynamic stochastic general equilibrium (DSGE) models that can be used for policy analysis. The recent class of models developed for this purpose has vastly more features than any simple RBC model, and a variety of techniques have been developed for the purpose of matching the model to the data. One can ask whether this class of models overcomes some of the criticisms leveled against the original RBC approach.

Consider, for example, the model recently proposed by Kapetanios, Pagan, and Scott [123] for policy analysis of a small open economy. According to them:

> [This] model is stark in its assumptions. There are no market frictions and no locational specificity. For example, there is no banking sector and no specific role for money and credit in the monetary transmission mechanism. There are no market frictions and distortions, no fixed costs or discontinuities. The model assumes a representative household and a symmetric equilibrium for firms. Above all, markets are assumed to clear at all times, as all agents have complete knowledge of the economy and complete understanding of shocks when they hit. In sum, the model contains assumptions that are almost guaranteed to be violated by the data, especially in the short run.

Yet this model has a core set of 26 equations!

As another example, consider the model proposed by Christiano, Eichenbaum, and Evans [67] for the analysis of the effects of monetary policy shocks on real and nominal variables. The aim of this model is to reproduce the inertial behavior of inflation and persistence in real quantities. To capture the first feature, the model incorporates wage and price contracts following the approach in Calvo [54]. The model also incorporates a variety of "real" frictions such as habit persistence in consumption, adjustment costs in investment, and variable capital utilization. Finally, firms are assumed to borrow working capital to finance their wage bill. There is also an interest-rate-setting rule that defines monetary policy. Christiano *et al.* [67] pursue a limited information estimation strategy by estimating a subset of the parameters of the model to match the impulse responses of eight key macroeconomic variables to a monetary policy shock with those implied from an identified VAR using the so-called method of *indirect inference*.[10] The authors' analysis is, in many ways, an exploratory analysis of the role of nominal and real rigidities in propagating shocks. It is also very much in the spirit of the original Kydland–Prescott approach [141] in that the goal is to match a set of observed characteristics — in this case, the impulse responses to a given monetary shock. Christiano *et al.* provide some evidence on the role of price and wage rigidities, but in a highly restrictive environment. For example, the model assumes a continuum of households which are heterogeneous in their wage and the hours that they work, but homogeneous in their consumption and asset holdings, with the latter result derived from the existence of state-contingent securities for consumption.

Christiano *et al.* [67] derive much of their evidence regarding the types of real rigidities on the results of calibration-type exercises of the current generation of macroeconomic models such as habit persistence or adjustment costs. However, there are shortcomings in their approach. For example, estimated models of adjustment costs have been shown to imply implausible degrees of costs of adjustment. Furthermore, the adjustment cost model has been criticized on the grounds that it implies a constant cost of adjustment which does not vary with economic conditions. By contrast, the irreversible investment model studied by Demers [78] and others has been shown to generate a time-varying adjustment cost that varies in response to changes in objective and subjective forms of risk and uncertainty.[11] Christiano *et al.* [67] assume that monetary policy shocks are drawn from a given and known distribution. Yet, one could also question the implications of the model should there be changes in the distribution of the exogenous processes. In such cases, the assumption of a constant adjustment cost parameter would fail to hold, implying that the propagation mechanisms would vary with changes in the distribution of exogenous variables facing agents. This raises

---

[10] For a recent example of the method of indirect inference applied to a model of the EU economy, see Meenagh, Minford, and Wickens [160].

[11] For a review and discussion, see also Demers, Demers, and Altug [79]. For applications, see Altug, Demers, and Demers [10, 11].

the issue of whether DSGE models are, in fact, structural or invariant to interventions.

Following the initial contribution of Altug [5], a variety of other papers have implemented maximum likelihood estimation of dynamic equilibrium models. McGrattan, Rogerson, and Wright [159] consider an equilibrium business cycle model with household production and distortionary taxation. As in the analysis of Altug [5], they augment the approximate linear laws of motion with additional shocks. However, they employ time domain methods by making use of the Kalman filter with a linear law of motion for the state variables and a linear measurement equation for a key set of observables. More recent applications include Canova [60] and Ireland [121], amongst others. The recent research on DSGE models has also employed Bayesian analysis as a way of incorporating prior uncertainty about the parameters of interest (see, for example, Schorfhiede [186] and An and Schorfhiede [15]). Similar to Canova [56], this approach first provides a link with the calibration approach by allowing the researcher to use information from microeconomic studies or macroeconometric estimates. Second, the use of Bayesian methods and, in particular, examining the posterior distribution calculated as the prior distribution times the likelihood function is often more straightforward computationally than maximizing the likelihood function, which is typically a high-dimensional object.

The Bayesian estimation of DSGE models involves several steps. First, the method presupposes that a solution can be found for the underlying economic model of interest. There are a variety of approaches for solving nonlinear dynamic stochastic models. Judd [122] provides a textbook treatment of many currently used solution methods. Second, the likelihood function for the observations must be formed. Third, the posterior distribution for the parameters, which is obtained from the prior distribution and the likelihood function, must be examined. To illustrate this approach, suppose that the state space representation for the model's solution consists of the following:

- a transition equation $S_t = g(S_{t-1}, v_t, \theta)$, where S_t is a vector of state variables that describe the evolution of the model over time, v_t is a vector of innovations, and θ is a vector of parameters characterizing preferences, the production technology, and information; and

- a measurement equation $Y_t = h(S_t, w_t, \theta)$, where Y_t are the observables and w_t are the shocks to the observables (which may take the form of measurement errors, among others).

This state space representation can be used to derive the likelihood function of the observables and to obtain the posterior distribution for the parameters conditional on the observations. Given the probability density functions for the shocks $f_v(\cdot)$ and $f_w(\cdot)$, we can also compute the probabilities $p(S_t|S_{t-1};\theta)$ and $p(Y_t|S_t;\theta)$. Notice that

$$Y_t = h(g(S_{t-1}, v_t, \theta), w_t, \theta).$$

Hence, we can compute $p(Y_t|S_{t-1};\theta)$. Likewise, the state space representation allows us to compute the likelihood of the observations $y^T = (y_1, \ldots, y_T)$ at the parameter values θ as

$$p(y^T;\theta) = p(y_1|\theta) \prod_{t=2}^{T} p(y_t|y^{t-1};\theta)$$

$$= \int p(S_1|S_0;\theta)dS_0 \prod_{t=2}^{T} \int p(Y_t|S_t;\theta)p(S_t|y^{t-1};\theta)dS_t.$$

Given a prior distribution $\pi(\theta)$ for the parameters θ, the posterior distribution can be expressed as

$$\pi(\theta|y^T) = \frac{p(y^T|\theta)\pi(\theta)}{\int p(y^T|\theta)\pi(\theta)d\theta}. \qquad (4.23)$$

The remaining task is to compute the sequence $\{p(S_t|y^{t-1};\theta)\}_{t=1}^{T}$, which shows the conditional distribution of the states given the observations. The excellent survey by Fernandez-Villaverde [90] describes in detail how to implement Bayesian estimation of DSGE models. Following his approach, this sequence is computed by making use of the relation[12]

$$p(S_{t+1}|y^t;\theta) = \int p(S_{t+1}|S_t;\theta)p(S_t|y^t;\theta)dS_t$$

---

[12]This is known as the Chapman–Kolmogorov equation.

and an application of Bayes' theorem as

$$p(S_t|y^t;\theta) = \frac{p(y_t|S_t;\theta)p(S_t|y^{t-1};\theta)}{\int p(y_t|S_t;\theta)p(S_t|y^{t-1};\theta)dS_t}.$$

Finding the posterior distribution of the parameters displayed in (4.23) involves a few remaining steps. First, if the transition and measurement equations are linear and if the shocks are normally distributed, then the Kalman filter is used to obtain the likelihood function. Otherwise, a method known as the particle filter[13] is used to evaluate the likelihood function. However, even if we can evaluate the posterior distribution, exploring it for different values of θ typically involves the use of sampling through Markov chain Monte Carlo (MCMC) methods.

Smets and Wouters [194, 195] provide two important examples of this approach. They extend the approach in Christiano *et al.* [67] to estimate the parameters of a DSGE model with real and nominal frictions for the euro area using Bayesian methods. In contrast to the approach in Christiano *et al.* [67], however, they consider a full set of structural shocks. These include a productivity shock, a labor supply shock, a shock to the household's discount factor, an investment-specific shock, and a government consumption shock plus three "cost-push" shocks. They consider the behavior of seven key macroeconomic time series in the euro area — real GDP, consumption, investment, the GDP deflator, the real wage, employment, and the nominal short-term interest rate — by minimizing the posterior distribution model's parameters based on a linearized state space representation for the model. Smets and Wouters [194] argue that their approach offers several important advances. First, they find that, based on Bayesian model evaluation criteria, the estimated DSGE model performs as well as standard and Bayesian VARs. Second, they find that the estimates of the structural parameters of the model are plausible and, on the whole, similar to those for the US economy. Their estimates imply more price stickiness than the estimates of Christiano *et al.* [67]. Third, they argue that the effects of the different shocks on the variables of interest are consistent with existing evidence that does not rely on a DSGE framework. For example, a temporary contractionary monetary shock has a temporary negative effect on output and inflation. Fourth, their findings attribute the largest role

---

[13] See Schorfhiede [186] or Fernandez-Villaverde [90].

to labor supply and monetary shocks in accounting for the variation in output in the euro area. One problem with this approach, as we discussed above, is that there tends to be a circularity in building a model to match findings, say, from a standard VAR, which may not be robust themselves.

In his survey written in 1992, Fair [86] expressed his disappointment with both the RBC and New Keynesian research agendas in the following way: "The RBC literature is interested in testing in only a very limited way, and the New Keynesian literature is not econometric enough to even talk about serious testing." In the last 20 years or so, the New Keynesian agenda has progressed much closer towards gaining an explicitly econometric focus. Yet, it is difficult to say how much headway has been made in understanding the propagation mechanisms underlying business cycle fluctuations. Simple models with features ranging from home production to government consumption shocks to nonseparable preferences have been examined to understand their inner workings, as have the roles of nominal rigidities and price-setting behavior. While these model features have proved useful for accounting for some stylized facts, they have often continued to retain counterfactual implications. For example, Cogley and Nason [70] show that the home production framework produces a negative autocorrelation for output. As discussed earlier, many of the model features, such as symmetric and constant adjustment costs in investment, are essentially *ad hoc* and are at variance with empirical evidence at the micro level. The recent DSGE models include a large set of shocks that have little economic meaning. By its very construction, the DSGE framework cannot easily move into a setup that relaxes the representative consumer assumption, be this through observed and unobserved forms of heterogeneity or the presence of uninsurable risk. Yet, even under the complete markets assumption, Altug and Miller [7, 8] show that exogenous and endogenous forms of heterogeneity matter for the behavior of individual allocations. Browning, Hansen, and Heckman [48] provide a comprehensive discussion regarding the role of heterogeneity in general equilibrium modeling, and raise cautionary points about linking the current class of dynamic equilibrium models that dominate macroeconomics with microeconomic models and evidence.

Could the entire general equilibrium macroeconomic quantitative theorizing approach — despite the use of much bigger models and more powerful computational tools — be a detour, as Fair [86] seems to indicate?

Should economists build intuition from the workings of well-articulated economic models at the same time as they use more purely econometric approaches for quantitative policy analysis? Kapetanios *et al.* [123] note that the current class of fully articulated dynamic equilibrium models that are increasingly being used by policy-makers such as central banks help to provide restrictions on a reduced form, a practice very much in the spirit of the Cowles Commission approach. Thus, the exercise is not necessarily to recover structure in the form of the parameters of preferences and technology, as argued by Lucas [150] in his famous critique of econometric policy evaluation. More tellingly, can economists hope to recover "true structure" using macroeconomic data in the presence of observed and unobserved forms of heterogeneity? Or, alternatively, when subjective beliefs by economic agents in a changing stochastic environment constitute "hidden structure", as Martin Weitzman [210] claims?

The notion that structural models may not indeed be structural has begun to be discussed in the literature. Fernandez-Villaverde and Rubio-Ramirez [91], for example, discuss the stability over time of estimated parameters in DSGE models, and show that the parameters characterizing the pricing behavior of households and firms in Calvo-type pricing functions are correlated with inflation. Canova and Sala [61] investigate identifiability issues in DSGE models and their consequences for parameter estimation and model evaluation when the objective function measures the distance between estimated and model impulse responses. They show that observational equivalence as well as partial and weak identification problems are widespread, lead to biased estimates and unreliable t-statistics, and may induce investigators to select false models. Canova [59] also examines the issue of identifiability of DSGE models, and argues that researchers should be careful in interpreting the diagnostics obtained from the estimation of structural models and make use of additional data in the form of micro data or data from other countries to augment the information obtained by formal estimation.

Chapter 8
Future Areas for Research

The literature on business cycles is vast. In this book, I have offered a perspective based on my own perceptions and mindsets. Nevertheless, even the experience of reviewing some of this literature shows that it is lively, at times contentious, but always thought-provoking. There are many other topics of interest that we could have discussed regarding business cycles. For one, I have omitted a discussion of multi-sector models in generating business cycle behavior. For example, it may be that shocks are concentrated in a particular sector and are propagated to the rest of the economy from that sector.[1] In such cases, one needs to consider multi-sector models since the one-sector growth model does not allow for a consideration of these issues. However, multi-sector models may also have shortcomings because they typically imply that overall expansions in the economy are associated with contractions in one sector.

More generally, I have not provided a discussion of models with self-fulfilling expectations and multiple equilibria. Farmer [87] provides an eloquent enunciation of this approach, and contrasts it with the standard real business cycle (RBC) approach. Many have argued that such models are more in the spirit of true Keynesianism because they stress the role of "animal spirits". In a recent analysis, Farmer [88] generates a model of self-fulfilling equilibria which arises from market failure associated with the labor market. Specifically, he considers the role of a search externality and a lemons problem in the market for search inputs. Many recent works assume that there is a search technology such that firms and workers are randomly matched; the wage is then set by a

---

[1] See, for example, Benhabib and Farmer [38].

Nash bargaining process.[2] In contrast to this literature, Farmer [88] drops the assumption that wages are determined as a result of a Nash bargaining process. Instead, he assumes that firms offer the same wage in advance. This leads to a model with a continuum of steady-state equilibria. In these equilibria, all firms earn zero profits but not all equilibria have the same welfare properties. This feature of the model allows for the role of "confidence", which is transmitted to real variables through investors' beliefs about the stock market. This leads to a *demand-constrained* equilibrium. The policy implications of such a model differ from those of the standard textbook Keynesian model, which seeks to alleviate demand-induced shortfalls in output through large fiscal stimuli. By contrast, the model with a search externality emphasizes the role of confidence in restoring full-employment output. Farmer [88] concludes his analysis by commenting on the potential efficacy of the Obama fiscal stimulus package(s) in light of the findings from his model.

This book has also omitted a discussion of models with credit and collateral constraints. One could argue that this type of model deserves much more attention given the global financial crisis that originated from the subprime housing market in the US in 2007.[3]

The above considerations show that business cycles will continue to be a topic of discussion among economists for many years to come. Undoubtedly, this discussion will be accompanied by the development of new models, new techniques, and new controversies regarding both. However, irrespective of what the new models or techniques will look like, we may conclude that the debate surrounding their development will not cease to arouse interest or to generate future avenues for research.

---

[2]This approach owes its origins to the analysis in Mortensen and Pissarides [165]. For a recent application in the context of a standard RBC model, see Cooley and Quadrini [76].

[3]For a recent analysis of models with financial frictions in a dynamic general equilibrium setting, see Pierrard, de Walque, and Rouabah [171].

Bibliography

1. Aguiar, M. and G. Gopinath (2004). "Emerging Market Business Cycles: The Trend Is the Cycle," *Journal of Political Economy*, 115, pp. 69–102.
2. A'Hearna, B. and U. Woitek (2001). "More International Evidence on the Historical Properties of Business Cycles," *Journal of Monetary Economics*, 47, pp. 321–346.
3. Ahmed, S. and R. Murthy (1994). "Money, Output, and Real Business Cycles in a Small Open Economy," *Canadian Journal of Economics*, 27, pp. 982–993.
4. Altug, S. (1985). "Gestation Lags and the Business Cycle," Unpublished manuscript.
5. Altug, S. (1989). "Time-to-Build and Aggregate Fluctuations: Some New Evidence," *International Economic Review*, 30, pp. 889–920.
6. Altug, S. and P. Labadie (2008). *Asset Pricing for Dynamic Economies*. Cambridge: Cambridge University Press.
7. Altug, S. and R. Miller (1990). "Household Choices in Equilibrium," *Econometrica*, 58, pp. 543–570.
8. Altug, S. and R. Miller (1998). "The Effect of Past Experience on Female Wages and Labor Supply," *Review of Economic Studies*, 65, pp. 45–85.
9. Altug, S., R. Ashley, and D. Patterson (1999). "Are Technology Shocks Nonlinear?" *Macroeconomic Dynamics*, 3, pp. 506–533.
10. Altug, S., F. Demers, and M. Demers (2007). "Political Risk and Irreversible Investment," *CESifo Economic Studies*, 53, pp. 430–465.
11. Altug, S., F. Demers, and M. Demers (2009). "The Investment Tax Credit and Irreversible Investment," *Journal of Macroeconomics*, forthcoming.
12. Alvarez, F. and U. Jermann (2000). "Efficiency, Equilibrium, and Asset Pricing with Risk of Default," *Econometrica*, 68, pp. 775–797.
13. Ambler, S., E. Cardia, and C. Zimmermann (2002). "International Transmission of the Business Cycle in a Multi-sector Model," *European Economic Review*, 46, pp. 273–300.
14. Ambler, S., E. Cardia, and C. Zimmermann (2004). "International Business Cycles: What Are the Facts?" *Journal of Monetary Economics*, 51, pp. 257–276.

15. An, S. and F. Schorfhiede (2007). "Bayesian Analysis of DSGE Models," *Econometric Reviews*, 26, pp. 113–172.

16. Anderson, E., L. Hansen, E. McGrattan, and T. Sargent (1996). "Mechanics of Forming and Estimating Dynamic Linear Economies," In H. Amman, D. Kendrick, and J. Rust (eds.), *Handbook of Computational Economics Vol. 1, Handbooks in Economics, Vol. 13*, Amsterdam: Elsevier Science/North-Holland, pp. 171–252.

17. Arellano, C. and E. Mendoza (2003). "Credit Frictions and 'Sudden Stops' in Small Open Economies: An Equilibrium Business Cycle Framework for Emerging Markets Crises," In S. Altug, J. Chadha, and C. Nolan (eds.), *Dynamic Macroeconomic Analysis: Theory and Policy in General Equilibrium*, Cambridge: Cambridge University Press, pp. 335–405.

18. Artis, M. and W. Zhang (1997). "International Business Cycles and the ERM: Is There a European Business Cycle?" *International Journal of Finance and Economics*, 2, pp. 1–16.

19. Artis, M. and W. Zhang (1999). "Further Evidence on the International Business Cycle and the ERM: Is There a European Business Cycle?" *Oxford Economic Papers*, 51, pp. 120–132.

20. Artis, M., Z. Kontolemis, and D. Osborn (1997). "Business Cycles for G7 and European Countries," *Journal of Business*, 70, pp. 249–279.

21. Artis, M., M. Marcellino, and T. Proietti (2003). "Dating the Euro Area Business Cycle," Innocenzo Gasparini Institute for Economic Research (IGIER) Working Paper No. 237.

22. Ashley, R. and D. Patterson (1989). "Linear versus Nonlinear Macroeconomics: A Statistical Test," *International Economic Review*, 30, pp. 685–704.

23. Backus, D. and P. Kehoe (1992). "International Evidence on the Historical Perspective of Business Cycles," *American Economic Review*, 82, pp. 864–888.

24. Backus, D. and G. Smith (1993). "Consumption and Real Exchange Rates in Dynamic Economies with Non-traded Goods," *Journal of International Economics*, 35, pp. 297–316.

25. Backus, D., P. Kehoe, and F. Kydland (1992). "International Real Business Cycles," *Journal of Political Economy*, 100, pp. 745–775.

26. Backus, D., P. Kehoe, and F. Kydland (1995). "International Business Cycles: Theory and Evidence," In T. Cooley (ed.), *Frontiers of Business Cycle Research*, Princeton: Princeton University Press, pp. 331–356.

27. Barro, R. (1987). "Government Spending, Interest Rates, Prices and Budget Deficits in the United Kingdom, 1701–1918," *Journal of Monetary Economics*, 20, pp. 221–247.

28. Barsky, R. and L. Kilian (2004). "Oil and the Macroeconomy Since the 1970s," *Journal of Economic Perspectives*, 18, pp. 115–134.

29. Basu, S. (1996). "Procyclical Productivity: Increasing Returns or Cyclical Utilization?" *Quarterly Journal of Economics*, 111, pp. 719–751.

30. Basu, S. and M. Kimball (1997). "Cyclical Productivity with Unobserved Input Variation," NBER Working Paper No. 5915.

31. Basu, S. and A. Taylor (1999). "Business Cycles in International Historical Perspective," *Journal of Economic Perspectives*, 13, pp. 45–68.

32. Basu, S., J. Fernald, and M. Kimball (2006). "Are Technology Improvements Contractionary?" *American Economic Review*, 96, pp. 1418–1448.

33. Baxter, M. (1995). "International Trade and Business Cycles," In G. Grossman and K. Rogoff (eds.), *Handbook of International Economics*, Amsterdam: North-Holland, pp. 1801–1864.

34. Baxter, M. and M. Crucini (1995). "Business Cycles and the Asset Structure of Foreign Trade," *International Economic Review*, 36, pp. 821–854.

35. Baxter, M. and D. Farr (2005). "Variable Factor Utilization and International Business Cycles," *Journal of International Economics*, 65, pp. 335–347.

36. Baxter, M. and U. Jermann (1997). "The International Diversification Puzzle Is Worse Than You Think," *American Economic Review*, 87(1), pp. 170–180.

37. Baxter, M. and R. King (1999). "Measuring Business Cycles: Approximate Band-pass Filters for Economic Time Series," *The Review of Economics and Statistics*, 81, pp. 575–593.

38. Benhabib, J. and R. Farmer (1996). "Indeterminacy and Sector-Specific Externalities," *Journal of Monetary Economics*, 37, pp. 421–443.

39. Benhabib, J., R. Rogerson, and R. Wright (1991). "Homework in Macroeconomics: Household Production and Aggregate Fluctuations," *Journal of Political Economy*, 99, pp. 1166–1187.

40. Bernanke, B. and M. Gertler (1989). "Agency Costs, Net Worth and Business Fluctuations," *American Economic Review*, 79, pp. 14–31.

41. Bernanke, B., M. Gertler, and S. Gilchrist (1996). "The Financial Accelerator and the Flight to Quality," *Review of Economics and Statistics*, 78, pp. 1–15.

42. Bertola, G. and R. Caballero (1994). "Irreversibility and Aggregate Investment," *Review of Economic Studies*, 61, pp. 223–246.

43. Blanchard, O. and D. Quah (1989). "The Dynamic Effects of Demand versus Supply Disturbances," *American Economic Review*, 79, pp. 654–673.

44. Bordo, M. and T. Heibling (2003). "Have National Business Cycles Become More Synchronized?" NBER Working Paper No. W10130.

45. Bowman, D. and B. Doyle (2003). "New Keynesian, Open-Economy Models and Their Implications for Monetary Policy," Federal Reserve Board (FRB) International Finance Discussion Paper No. 2003-762.

46. Braun, A. (1994). "Tax Disturbances and Real Activity in the Postwar United States," *Journal of Monetary Economics*, 33, pp. 441–462.

47. Brock, W. and C. Sayers (1988). "Is the Business Cycle Characterized by Deterministic Chaos?" *Journal of Monetary Economics*, 22, pp. 71–90.

48. Browning, M., L. Hansen, and J. Heckman (1999). "Micro Data and General Equilibrium Models," In J. Taylor and M. Woodford (eds.), *Handbook of Macroeconomics, Vol. 1A*, Amsterdam: Elsevier Science, Ch. 8.

49. Bry, G. and C. Boschan (1971). *Cyclical Analysis of Time Series: Selected Procedures and Computer Programs*. New York: Columbia University Press for the NBER.

50. Burns, A. and W. Mitchell (1946). *Measuring Business Cycles*. New York: NBER.

51. Burnside, C. and M. Eichenbaum (1996). "Factor Hoarding and the Propagation of Business Cycle Shocks," *American Economic Review*, 86, pp. 1154–1174.

52. Burnside, C., M. Eichenbaum, and S. Rebelo (1993). "Labor Hoarding and the Business Cycle," *Journal of Political Economy*, 101, pp. 245–274.

53. Caballero, R. (1999). "Aggregate Investment," In J. Taylor and M. Woodford (eds.), *Handbook of Macroeconomics, Vol. 1B*, North Holland: Elsevier Science, Ch. 12.

54. Calvo, G. (1983). "Staggered Prices in a Utility-Maximizing Framework," *Journal of Monetary Economics*, 12, pp. 383–398.

55. Campbell, J. (1994). "Inspecting the Mechanism: An Analytical Approach to the Stochastic Growth Model," *Journal of Monetary Economics*, 33, pp. 463–506.
56. Canova, F. (1994). "Statistical Inference in Calibrated Models," *Journal of Applied Econometrics*, 9, pp. 123–144.
57. Canova, F. (1995). "Sensitivity Analysis and Model Evaluation in Simulated Dynamic General Equilibrium Economies," *International Economic Review*, 36, pp. 477–501.
58. Canova, F. (2006). *Methods for Applied Macroeconomic Analysis*. Princeton: Princeton University Press.
59. Canova, F. (2008). "How Much Structure in Empirical Models?" CEPR Discussion Paper No. 6791.
60. Canova, F. (2009). "What Explains the Great Moderation in the US? A Structural Analysis," *Journal of the European Economic Association*, 7, pp. 697–721.
61. Canova, F. and L. Sala (2006). "Back to Square One: Identification Issues in DSGE Models," ECB Working Paper No. 583.
62. Chadha, J. and C. Nolan (2002). "A Long View of the UK Business Cycle," *National Institute Economic Review*, 182, pp. 72–89.
63. Chari, V., P. Kehoe, and E. McGrattan (2004). "Are Structural VARs Useful Guides for Developing Business Cycle Theories?" Federal Reserve Bank of Minneapolis Research Department Working Paper No. 631.
64. Christiano, L. (1988). "Why Does Inventory Investment Fluctuate So Much?" *Journal of Monetary Economics*, 21, pp. 247–280.
65. Christiano, L. and M. Eichenbaum (1992). "Current Real Business Cycle Theories and Aggregate Labor Market Fluctuations," *American Economic Review*, 82, pp. 430–450.
66. Christiano, L., M. Eichenbaum, and C. Evans (1997). "Sticky Price and Limited Participation Models of Money: A Comparison," *European Economic Review*, 41, pp. 1201–1249.
67. Christiano, L., M. Eichenbaum, and C. Evans (2005). "Nominal Rigidities and the Dynamic Effects of a Shock to Monetary Policy," *Journal of Political Economy*, 113, pp. 1–45.
68. Christiano, L., M. Eichenbaum, and R. Vigfusson (2003). "What Happens After a Technology Shock?" NBER Working Paper No. 9819.
69. Cogley, T. and J. Nason (1995). "Effects of the Hodrick–Prescott Filter on Trend and Difference Stationary Time Series: Implications for Business Cycle Research," *Journal of Economic Dynamics and Control*, 19, pp. 253–278.
70. Cogley, T. and J. Nason (1995). "Output Dynamics in Real Business Cycle Models," *American Economic Review*, 85, pp. 492–511.
71. Cole, H. (1988). "Financial Structure and International Trade," *International Economic Review*, 29, pp. 237–259.
72. Cole, H. and M. Obstfeld (1991). "Commodity Trade and International Risk Sharing," *Journal of Monetary Economics*, 28, pp. 3–24.
73. Coleman, W. (1997). "The Behavior of Interest Rates in a General Equilibrium Multi-sector Model with Irreversible Investment," *Macroeconomic Dynamics*, 1, pp. 206–227.
74. Cooley, T. (ed.) (1995). *Frontiers of Business Cycle Research*. Princeton: Princeton University Press.
75. Cooley, T. and E. Prescott (1995). "Economic Growth and Business Cycles," In T. Cooley (ed.), *Frontiers of Business Cycle Research*, Princeton: Princeton University Press, pp. 1–38.

76. Cooley, T. and V. Quadrini (1999). "A Neoclassical Model of the Phillips Curve Relation," *Journal of Monetary Economics*, 44, pp. 165–193.

77. Correia, I., J. Neves, and S. Rebelo (1995). "Business Cycles in Small Open Economies," *European Economic Review*, 39, pp. 1089–1113.

78. Demers, M. (1991). "Irreversibility and the Arrival of Information," *Review of Economic Studies*, 58, pp. 333–350.

79. Demers, F., M. Demers, and S. Altug (2003). "Investment Dynamics," In S. Altug, J. Chadha, and C. Nolan (eds.), *Dynamic Macroeconomic Analysis: Theory and Policy in General Equilibrium*, Cambridge: Cambridge University Press, pp. 34–154.

80. Denison, E. (1985). *Trends in American Economic Growth, 1929–1982*. Washington, DC: Brookings.

81. Devereux, M., A. Gregory, and G. Smith (1992). "Realistic Cross-Country Consumption Correlations in a Two-Country, Equilibrium Business Cycle Model," *Journal of International Money and Finance*, 11, pp. 3–16.

82. Eichenbaum, M. (1991). "Real Business Cycles: Wisdom or Whimsy?" *Journal of Economic Dynamics and Control*, 15, pp. 607–626.

83. Eichenbaum, M., L. Hansen, and K. Singleton (1988). "A Time Series Analysis of Representative Agent Models of Consumption and Leisure Choice Under Uncertainty," *Quarterly Journal of Economics*, 103, pp. 51–78.

84. Eichengreen, B. and M. Bordo (2002). "Crises Now and Then: What Lessons from the Last Era of Financial Globalization?" NBER Working Paper No. W8716.

85. Fagan, G., J. Henry, and R. Mestre (2001). "An Area-Wide Model (AWM) for the Euro Area," ECB Working Paper No. 42.

86. Fair (1992). "The Cowles Commission Approach, Real Business Cycle Theories, and New Keynesian Economics," Cowles Foundation Discussion Paper No. 1004.

87. Farmer, R. (1999). *The Macroeconomics of Self-Fulfilling Prophecies*, 2nd ed. Cambridge, MA: MIT Press.

88. Farmer, R. (2009). "Confidence, Crashes, and Animal Spirits," NBER Working Paper No. 14846.

89. Feldstein, M. and C. Horioka (1980). "Domestic Saving and International Capital Flows," *Economic Journal*, 90, pp. 314–329.

90. Fernandez-Villaverde, J. (2009). "The Econometrics of DSGE Models," NBER Working Paper No. 14677.

91. Fernandez-Villaverde, J. and R. Rubio-Ramirez (2007). "How Structural Are Structural Parameters?" NBER Working Paper No. 13166.

92. Finn, M. (2000). "Perfect Competition and the Effects of Energy Price Increases on Economic Activity," *Journal of Money, Credit, and Banking*, 32, pp. 400–416.

93. Forni, M. and L. Reichlin (1998). "Let's Get Real: A Factor Analytical Approach to Disaggregated Business Cycle Dynamics," *Review of Economic Studies*, 65, pp. 453–473.

94. Friedman, M. and A. Schwartz (1963). *A Monetary History of the United States, 1867–1960*. Princeton: Princeton University Press.

95. Frisch, R. (1933). "Propagation Problems and Impulse Problems in Dynamic Economies," In *Economic Essays in Honor of Gustav Cassel*, London: George Allen & Unwin.

96. Gali, J. (1999). "Technology, Employment, and the Business Cycle: Do Technology Shocks Explain Aggregate Fluctuations?" *American Economic Review*, 89, pp. 249–271.

97. Gali, J. (2008). *Monetary Policy, Inflation, and the Business Cycle*. Princeton: Princeton University Press.

98. Gali, J. and P. Rabanal (2005). "Technology Shocks and Aggregate Fluctuations: How Well Does the RBC Model Fit Postwar US Data?" In M. Gertler and K. Rogoff (eds.), *NBER Macroeconomics Annual 2004*, Cambridge, MA: MIT Press, pp. 225–318.

99. Gallant, R. and G. Tauchen (1996). "Which Moments to Match?" *Econometric Theory*, 12, pp. 657–681.

100. Gallant, R. and G. Tauchen (1998). "SNP: A Program for Nonparametric Time Series Analysis, Version 8.7, User's Guide," University of North Carolina Working Paper.

101. Garcia-Cicco, J., R. Pancrazi, and M. Uribe (2006). "Real Business Cycles in Emerging Countries?" NBER Working Paper No. 12629.

102. Geweke, J. (1999). "Computational Experiments and Reality," SCE Computing in Economics and Finance Working Paper No. 401.

103. Giannone, D., L. Reichlin, and L. Sala (2006). "VARs, Common Factors and the Empirical Validation of Equilibrium Business Cycle Models," *Journal of Econometrics*, 132, pp. 257–279.

104. Gordon, R. (1990). *The Measurement of Durable Goods Prices*. Chicago: University of Chicago Press.

105. Greenwood, J., Z. Hercowitz, and G. Huffman (1988). "Investment, Capacity Utilization, and the Real Business Cycle," *American Economic Review*, 78, pp. 402–417.

106. Greenwood, J., Z. Hercowitz, and P. Krusell (1997). "Long-Run Implications of Investment-Specific Technological Change," *American Economic Review*, 87, pp. 342–362.

107. Greenwood, J., Z. Hercowitz, and P. Krusell (2000). "The Role of Investment-Specific Technological Change in the Business Cycle," *European Economic Review*, 44, pp. 91–115.

108. Gregory, A. and A. Smith (1989). "Calibration as Estimation," *Econometric Reviews*, 9, pp. 57–89.

109. Gregory, A., A. Head, and J. Raynauld (1997). "Measuring World Business Cycles," *International Economic Review*, 38, pp. 677–702.

110. Hall, R. (1988). "The Relation Between Price and Marginal Cost in U.S. Industry," *Journal of Political Economy*, 96, pp. 921–947.

111. Hall, R. (1990). "Invariance Properties of Solow's Productivity Residual," In P. Diamond (ed.), *Growth/Productivity/Unemployment*, Cambridge, MA: MIT Press, pp. 71–112.

112. Hansen, G. (1985). "Indivisible Labor and the Business Cycle," *Journal of Monetary Economics*, 16, pp. 309–327.

113. Hansen, L. (1982). "Large Sample Properties of Generalized Method of Moments Estimators," *Econometrica*, 50, pp. 1029–1054.

114. Hansen, L. and T. Sargent (1980). "Formulating and Estimating Dynamic Linear Rational Expectations Models," *Journal of Economic Dynamics and Control*, 2, pp. 7–46.

115. Harding, D. and A. Pagan (2003). "A Comparison of Business Cycle Dating Methods," *Journal of Economic Dynamics and Control*, 27, pp. 1681–1690.

116. Hartley, J., K. Hoover, and K. Salyer (eds.) (1998). *Real Business Cycles: A Reader*. London: Routledge.

117. Heathcote, J. and F. Perri (2002). "Financial Autarky and International Business Cycles," *Journal of Monetary Economics*, 49, pp. 601–627.

118. Helliwell, J. (1998). *How Much Do National Borders Matter?* Washington, DC: Brookings Institution.

119. Hess, G. and K. Shin (1997). "International and Intranational Business Cycles," *Oxford Review of Economic Policy*, 13, pp. 93–109.

120. Hodrick, R. and E. Prescott (1997). "Postwar U.S. Business Cycles," *Journal of Money, Credit, and Banking*, 29, pp. 1–16.

121. Ireland, P. (2004). "Technology Shocks in the New Keynesian Model," *Review of Economics and Statistics*, 86, pp. 923–936.

122. Judd, K. (1998). *Numerical Methods in Economics*. Cambridge, MA: MIT Press.

123. Kapetanios, G., A. Pagan, and A. Scott (2007). "Making a Match: Combining Theory and Evidence in Policy-Oriented Macroeconomic Modeling," *Journal of Econometrics*, 136, pp. 565–594.

124. Kehoe, T. and D. Levine (1993). "Debt Constrained Asset Markets," *Review of Economic Studies*, 60, pp. 865–888.

125. Kehoe, T. and D. Levine (2001). "Liquidity Constrained Markets versus Debt Constrained Markets," *Econometrica*, 69(3), pp. 575–598.

126. Kehoe, P. and F. Perri (2002). "International Business Cycles with Endogenous Incomplete Markets," *Econometrica*, 70, pp. 907–928.

127. Keynes, J. M. (1936). *The General Theory of Employment, Interest, and Money*. London: Macmillan.

128. King, R. (1995). "Quantitative Theory and Econometrics," *Economic Quarterly*, 81, pp. 53–105.

129. King, R. and C. Plosser (1984). "Money, Credit, and Prices in a Real Business Cycle Model," *American Economic Review*, 74, pp. 363–380.

130. King, R. and S. Rebelo (1993). "Low Frequency Filtering and Real Business Cycles," *Journal of Economic Dynamics and Control*, 17, pp. 207–231.

131. King, R., C. Plosser, and S. Rebelo (1988). "Production, Growth, and Business Cycles: I. The Basic Neoclassical Model," *Journal of Monetary Economics*, 21, pp. 195–232.

132. King, R., C. Plosser, and S. Rebelo (1988). "Production, Growth, and Business Cycles: II. New Directions," *Journal of Monetary Economics*, 21, pp. 309–341.

133. King, R., C. Plosser, J. Stock, and M. Watson (1991). "Stochastic Trends and Economic Fluctuations," *American Economic Review*, 81, pp. 819–840.

134. Kiyotaki, N. and J. Moore (1997). "Credit Cycles," *Journal of Political Economy*, 105, pp. 211–248.

135. Kocherlakota, N. (1996). "Implications of Efficient Risk Sharing without Commitment," *Review of Economic Studies*, 63, pp. 595–609.

136. Kollman, R. (1995). "Consumption, Real Exchange Rates, and the Structure of International Asset Markets," *Journal of International Money and Finance*, 14, pp. 191–211.

137. Kondratiev, N. (1926). "Die Langen Wellen der Konjunktur [The Long Waves of the Business Cycle]," *Archiv für Sozialwissenschaft und Sozialpolitik*, 56, pp. 573–606.

138. Köse, A., C. Otrok, and C. Whiteman (2003). "International Business Cycles: World, Region, and Country-Specific Factors," *American Economic Review*, 93, pp. 1216–1239.

139. Köse, A., E. Prasad, and M. Terrones (2003). "How Does Globalization Affect the Synchronization of Business Cycles?" IZA Discussion Paper No. 702.

140. Kydland, F. (1995). "Business Cycles and Aggregate Labor Market Fluctuations," In T. Cooley (ed.), *Frontiers of Business Cycle Research*, Princeton: Princeton University Press, pp. 126–156.

141. Kydland, F. and E. Prescott (1982). "Time-to-Build and Aggregate Fluctuations," *Econometrica*, 50, pp. 1345–1370.

142. Kydland, F. and E. Prescott (1990). "Business Cycles: Real Facts and a Monetary Myth," *Federal Reserve Bank of Minneapolis Quarterly Review*, 14, pp. 3–18.

143. Kydland, F. and E. Prescott (1991). "The Econometrics of the General Equilibrium Approach to Business Cycles," *Scandinavian Journal of Econometrics*, 93, pp. 161–178.

144. Kydland, F. and C. E. J. M. Zaragaza (2002). "Argentina's Lost Decade," *Review of Economic Dynamics*, 5, pp. 152–165.

145. Lewis, K. (1996). "What Can Explain the Apparent Lack of International Consumption Risk Sharing?" *Journal of Political Economy*, 104(2), pp. 267–297.

146. Ljungqvist, L. and T. Sargent (2000). *Recursive Macroeconomic Theory*. Cambridge, MA: MIT Press.

147. Long, J. and C. Plosser (1983). "Real Business Cycles," *Journal of Political Economy*, 91, pp. 39–69.

148. Lucas, R. (1972). "Expectations and the Neutrality of Money," *Journal of Economic Theory*, 4, pp. 103–123.

149. Lucas, R. (1975). "An Equilibrium Model of the Business Cycle," *Journal of Political Economy*, 83, pp. 1113–1144.

150. Lucas, R. (1976). "Econometric Policy Evaluation: A Critique," *Journal of Monetary Economics*, 1(2) (Supplementary Series), pp. 19–46.

151. Lucas, R. (1977). "Understanding Business Cycles," In K. Brunner and A. Meltzer (eds.), *Stabilization of the Domestic and International Economy*, Amsterdam: North-Holland, pp. 7–29.

152. Lucas, R. (1982). "Interest Rates and Currency Prices in a Two-Country World," *Journal of Monetary Economics*, 10, pp. 335–359.

153. Lucas, R. and L. Rapping (1969). "Real Wages, Employment and Inflation," *Journal of Political Economy*, 77, pp. 721–754.

154. Lumsdaine, R. and E. Prasad (2003). "Identifying the Common Component in International Economic Fluctuations," *Economic Journal*, 113, pp. 101–127.

155. Marcet, A. and R. Marimon (1999). "Recursive Contracts," Universitat Pompeu Fabra (UPF) Economics Working Paper No. 337.

156. McCallum, B. (1986). "On 'Real' and 'Sticky-Price' Theories of the Business Cycle," *Journal of Money, Credit, and Banking*, 18, pp. 397–414.

157. McCallum, J. (1996). "National Borders Matter: Canada-US Regional Trade Patterns," *American Economic Review*, 85, pp. 615–623.

158. McGrattan, E. (1994). "The Macroeconomic Effects of Distortionary Taxation," *Journal of Monetary Economics*, 33, pp. 573–601.

159. McGrattan, E., R. Rogerson, and R. Wright (1997). "An Equilibrium Model of the Business Cycle with Household Production and Fiscal Policy," *International Economic Review*, 38, pp. 267–290.

160. Meenagh, D., P. Minford, and M. Wickens (2008). "Testing a DSGE Model of the EU Using Indirect Inference," Cardiff Business School Economics Working Paper No. E2008/11.

161. Meese, R. and K. Rogoff (1983). "Empirical Exchange Rate Models of the Seventies: Do They Fit Out of Sample?" *Journal of International Economics*, 14, pp. 3–24.

162. Mendoza, E. (1991). "Real Business Cycles in a Small Open Economy," *American Economic Review*, 81, pp. 797–818.

163. Mitchell, W. (1927). *Business Cycles: The Problem and Its Setting.* New York: National Bureau of Economic Research.

164. Mitchell, W. and A. Burns (1938). *Statistical Indicators of Cyclical Revivals* (NBER Bulletin No. 69). New York: National Bureau of Economic Research.

165. Mortensen, D. and C. Pissarides (1994). "Job Creation and Job Destruction in the Theory of Unemployment," *Review of Economic Studies*, 61, pp. 391–415.

166. Neftci, S. (1984). "Are Economic Time Series Symmetric over the Business Cycle?" *Journal of Political Economy*, 92, pp. 307–328.

167. Nelson, C. and C. Plosser (1982). "Trends and Random Walks in Macroeconomic Time Series," *Journal of Monetary Economics*, 10, pp. 139 162.

168. Obstfeld, M. and K. Rogoff (2001). "The Six Major Puzzles in International Macroeconomics: Is There a Common Cause?" In B. Bernanke and K. Rogoff (eds.), *NBER Macroeconomics Annual 2000*, Cambridge, MA: MIT Press, pp. 339–390.

169. Ohanian, L. (1997). "The Macroeconomic Effects of War Finance in the United States: World War II and the Korean War," *American Economic Review*, 87, pp. 23–40.

170. Phelps, E. (1970). *Microeconomic Foundations of Employment and Inflation Theory.* New York: W.W. Norton & Co.

171. Pierrard, O., G. de Walque, and A. Rouabah (2008). "Financial (In)stability, Supervision and Liquidity Injections: A Dynamic General Equilibrium Approach," Unpublished manuscript.

172. Potter, S. (1999). "Nonlinear Time Series Modelling: An Introduction," *Journal of Economic Surveys*, 13, pp. 505–528.

173. Prescott, E. (1986). "Theory Ahead of Business Cycle Measurement," *Carnegie-Rochester Conference Series on Public Policy*, 25, pp. 11–44.

174. Ramey, V. and M. Shapiro (2001). "Displaced Capital: A Study of Aerospace Plant Closings," *Journal of Political Economy*, 109, pp. 958–992.

175. Ratfai, A. and P. Benczur (2005). "Economic Fluctuations in Central and Eastern Europe: The Facts," CEPR Discussion Paper No. 4846.

176. Ratfai, A. and P. Benczur (2008). "Facts of Business Cycles Around the Globe," Paper presented at the IEA 15th World Congress, Istanbul, Turkey.

177. Rebelo, S. (2005). "Real Business Models: Past, Present, and Future," *Scandinavian Journal of Economics*, 107, pp. 217–238.

178. Rodrik, D. (1991). "Policy Uncertainty and Private Investment in Developing Countries," *Journal of Development Economics*, 36, pp. 229–242.

179. Rogerson, R. (1988). "Indivisible Labor, Lotteries and Equilibrium," *Journal of Monetary Economics*, 21, pp. 3–16.

180. Romer, C. (1986). "Is the Stabilization of the Postwar Economy a Figment of the Data?" *American Economic Review*, 76, pp. 316–334.

181. Romer, C. (1989). "The Prewar Business Cycle Reconsidered: New Estimates of GNP, 1869–1908," *Journal of Political Economy*, 97, pp. 1–37.

182. Rotemberg, J. and M. Woodford (1995). "Dynamic General Equilibrium Models of Imperfectly Competitive Product Markets," In T. Cooley (ed.), *Frontiers of Business Cycle Research*, Princeton: Princeton University Press, pp. 243–293.

183. Rotemberg, J. and M. Woodford (1996). "Imperfect Competition and the Effects of Energy Price Increases on Economic Activity," *Journal of Money, Credit, and Banking*, 28, pp. 549–577.

184. Sargent, T. (1989). "Two Models of Measurement Error and the Investment Accelerator," *Journal of Political Economy*, 97, pp. 251–287.

185. Sargent, T. and C. Sims (1977). "Business Cycle Modeling Without Pretending to Have Too Much *A Priori* Economic Theory," In *New Methods in Business Cycle Research: Proceedings from a Conference*, Minneapolis, MN: Federal Reserve Bank of Minneapolis, pp. 45–109.

186. Schorfhiede, F. (2000). "Loss Function-based Evaluation of DSGE Models," *Journal of Applied Econometrics*, 15, pp. 645–670.

187. Schumpeter, J. (1934). *The Theory of Economic Growth*. Cambridge, MA: Harvard University Press.

188. Schumpeter, J. (1939). *Business Cycles*. New York: McGraw-Hill.

189. Serven, L. and A. Solimano (1993). "Private Investment and Macroeconomic Adjustment: A Survey," In L. Serven and A. Solimano (eds.), *Striving for Growth After Adjustment: The Role of Capital Formation*, Washington, DC: The World Bank, pp. 11–30.

190. Sims, C. (1972). "Money, Income and Causality," *American Economic Review*, 62, pp. 540–553.

191. Sims, C. (1980). "Macroeconomics and Reality," *Econometrica*, 48, pp. 1–48.

192. Singleton, K. (1988). "Econometric Issues in the Analysis of Equilibrium Business Cycle Models," *Journal of Monetary Economics*, 21, pp. 361–387.

193. Slutsky, E. (1937). "The Summation of Random Causes as the Source of Cyclic Processes," *Econometrica*, 5, pp. 105–146.

194. Smets, F. and R. Wouters (2003). "An Estimated Dynamic Stochastic General Equilibrium Model of the Euro Area," *Journal of the European Economic Association*, 1, pp. 1123–1175.

195. Smets, F. and R. Wouters (2005). "Comparing Shocks and Frictions in US and Euro Area Business Cycles: A Bayesian DSGE Approach," *Journal of Applied Econometrics*, 20, pp. 161–183.

196. Solow, R. (1957). "Technical Change and the Aggregate Production Function," *Review of Economics and Statistics*, 39, pp. 312–320.

197. Stock, J. and M. Watson (1999). "Business Cycle Fluctuations in U.S. Macroeconomic Time Series," In J. Taylor and M. Woodford (eds.), *Handbook of Macroeconomics, Vol. 1A*, North Holland: Elsevier Science, pp. 3–64.

198. Stock, J. and M. Watson (2003). "Has the Business Cycle Changed and Why?" In M. Gertler and K. Rogoff (eds.), *NBER Macroeconomics Annual 2002*, Cambridge, MA: MIT Press, pp. 159–230.

199. Stock, J. and M. Watson (2005). "Understanding Changes in International Business Cycle Dynamics," *Journal of the European Economic Association*, 5, pp. 968–1006.

200. Stockman, A. and L. Tesar (1995). "Tastes and Technology in a Two-Country Model of the Business Cycle: Explaining International Comovements," *American Economic Review*, 85, pp. 168–185.

201. Stokey, N. and R. Lucas, with E. Prescott (1989). *Recursive Methods in Economic Dynamics*. Cambridge, MA: Harvard University Press.

202. Summers, L. (1986). "Some Skeptical Observations on Real Business Cycle Theory," *Federal Reserve Bank of Minneapolis Quarterly Review*, 10, pp. 23–27.

203. Tesar, L. and I. Werner (1998). "The Internationalization of Securities Markets Since the 1987 Crash," In R. Litan and A. Santomero (eds.), *Brookings-Wharton Papers on Financial Services, Vol. 1*, Washington, DC: The Brookings Institution, pp. 281–372.

204. The Royal Swedish Academy of Sciences (2004). *Finn Kydland and Edward Prescott's Contribution to Dynamic Macroeconomics: The Time Consistency of Economic Policy and the Driving Forces Behind Business Cycles*. Advance Report on the Bank of Sweden Prize in Economic Sciences in Memory of Alfred Nobel.

205. Thomas, J. (2002). "Is Lumpy Investment Relevant for the Business Cycle?" *Journal of Political Economy*, 110, pp. 508–534.

206. Uhlig, H. (1997). "A Toolkit for Analyzing Nonlinear Dynamic Stochastic Models Easily," Available at http://www2.wiwi.hu-berlin.de/institute/wpol/html/toolkit.htm/.

207. Valderrama, D. (2007). "Statistical Nonlinearities in the Business Cycle: A Challenge for the Canonical RBC Model," *Journal of Economic Dynamics and Control*, 31(9), pp. 2957–2983.

208. Veracierto, M. (2002). "Plant-Level Irreversible Investment and Equilibrium Business Cycles," *American Economic Review*, 92, pp. 181–197.

209. Watson, M. (1993). "Measures of Fit for Calibrated Models," *Journal of Political Economy*, 101, pp. 1011–1041.

210. Weitzman, M. (2007). "Subjective Expectations and Asset-Return Puzzles," *American Economic Review*, 97, pp. 1102–1130.

211. Zarnowitz, V. (1992). *Business Cycles: Theory, History, Indicators, and Forecasting*. Chicago: The University of Chicago Press.

Index